李四光画传
（第三版）

1889—1971

J. S. Lee
A Picture Chronology
(The Third Edition)

《李四光画传（第三版）》编辑组 编

地质出版社
·北京·

《李四光画传（第三版）》编辑组

陈　群　周国均　邹宗平　徐　勇

高　平　余浩科　严春华　赵　曼

李四光画传（第三版）

1889—1971

J. S. Lee

A Picture Chronology

(The Third Edition)

序

Preface

李四光是世界著名的科学家，是中国现代地质学的开拓者和新中国地质事业的主要奠基人，是中国先进知识分子的杰出代表。他开创性、系统性地研究了中国的䗴业目古生物化石；发现和研究了中国的第四纪冰川；创建了地质力学学科，为地质找矿工作开辟了新途径。他曾担任全国政协副主席，首任地质部部长，兼任中央地震工作领导小组组长、国务院科教组组长、中国科学技术协会主席、全国科学规划委员会副主任、中国科学院副院长、中国科学院原子能委员会主任委员等职，领导全国地质找矿、地质调查研究工作，参加《科学技术发展远景规划纲要》编制工作，组织指导石油地质工作，并为建立我国能源材料基地、发展我国核事业、开展地震预报、开发地热资源等做出了重大贡献。毛泽东、周恩来、邓小平等老一辈党和国家领导人对李四光给予高度评价，称赞李四光是“一面旗帜”。

李四光一生不仅给我们留下了珍贵的科学遗产，而且给我们留下了宝贵的精神财富。这就是他始终不渝热爱祖国的赤子之心，忠于党和社会主义事业的高尚情操，振兴中华、造福人民的宏大志向，正直诚实、刚毅自强的优良品质和坚持真理、实事求是、勇于创新的科学精神。这笔精神财富，对我们做好新时期地质找矿工作，对建设中国特色社会主义事业具有十分重要的现实意义。

《李四光画传》以大量珍贵的历史照片，再现了李四光不平凡的一生。同时，也从一个侧面展示了新中国成立后地质找矿工作取得的巨大成就，再现了我国地质事业从小到大、从弱到强，成为国家经济社会发展重要支柱的光辉历程。

《李四光画传》的面世，既是对李四光诞辰120周年的很好纪念和对李四光光辉一生的深切缅怀，也是为庆祝中华人民共和国成立60周年献上的一份珍贵礼物。

徐绍史

2009年9月

出版说明

Imprint

李四光是中国现代地质学的开拓者和新中国地质事业的主要奠基人之一，是我国卓越的科学家、杰出的教育家、著名的社会活动家和伟大的爱国主义者。李四光把一生献给祖国和人民、献给科学事业，他以满腔的爱国热情，求真务实、开拓创新、无私奉献，为中国地质事业的发展立下不朽功勋。我们大力弘扬李四光精神，就是学习科学家们胸怀祖国、服务人民的爱国精神，勇攀高峰、敢为人先的创新精神，追求真理、严谨治学的求实精神，淡泊名利、潜心研究的奉献精神，集智攻关、团结协作的协同精神，甘为人梯、奖掖后学的育人精神。值此李四光诞辰135周年之际，我们再次修订出版这部画传，以寄托对他的深切缅怀和无限崇敬之情。

作为一部画传，需要图文并茂。李四光大半生在战火中度过，由于四处奔波，留下的图片资料甚少，在抗战期间又经历了从庐山到桂林、又从桂林到重庆的两次逃难，私人物品几乎全部丢失，其中就包括李四光早年的一些照片和重要档案资料。新中国成立后，在李四光肩负重任的20余年时间里，能收集到的工作照也十分有限。入选本画传的300余幅照片，主要由李四光亲属提供，十分珍贵；本画传同时还收录了李四光的部分手迹和档案资料，以及从人民出版社1984年出版的《李四光传》中摘录、编辑的文字。此次再版更正了第一、二版《李四光画传》（第一版：中国大地出版社2009年9月出版；第二版：中国大地出版社2015年10月出版）中的疏漏，更换、增加了李四光纪念馆等照片，以期形象、生动、准确地反映李四光艰辛探索、不懈奋斗的光辉一生。

这里，我们要衷心感谢自然资源部、中国地质调查局、李四光地质科学奖基金会对出版工作的指导与支持，感谢地质出版社为画传出版付出的辛勤劳动。

我们还要说明的是，新中国成立后李四光的部分照片由原中华人民共和国地质部工作人员及新华社记者拍摄。由于事隔多年，这些拍摄者或提供者的姓名难以确认，画传中未做明确标注，在此深表歉意。

《李四光画传（第三版）》编辑组

2024年10月于北京

目录
Contents

艰辛与光辉的历程

Struggles and Successes

李四光，字仲揆，湖北黄冈县（今黄冈市）人，生于1889年10月26日，卒于1971年4月29日。

李四光出身于贫寒的农村私塾教师家庭，少年时即聪慧好学，勤于思考，富有探索和创新精神，且宅心仁厚，立志报国。

他13岁考入武昌第二高等小学堂。15岁赴日留学，选攻造船专业。16岁加入孙中山领导的中国同盟会，并牢记孙先生的教导："努力向学，蔚为

1908年在日本大阪高等工业学校造船机械专业学习。

新中国成立后，李四光冲破敌对势力的阻挠，于1950年春回到祖国怀抱。同年任中国科学院副院长、地质工作计划指导委员会主任委员，主持召开全国地质工作会议。1952年成立地质部，李四光任地质部部长。后兼任全国科学规划委员会副主任、中国科学院原子能委员会主任委员、中央地震工作领导小组组长等，曾担任中华自然科学专门学会联合会主席、世界科学工作者协会执行委员会副主席、中国科学技术协会主席、中国人民政治协商会议全国委员会副主席等职。他参加编制《科学技术发展远景规划纲要》；向世界权威和“中国贫油”论发起挑战，组织和指导勘探开发石油及其他国家急需矿产资源，取得骄人成果，找到大油田，为中国摘掉了“贫油”帽子；找到其他重要矿藏，强力支撑了新中国的国民经济建设需要；部署和开展全国地质教育、科研和生产工作；高瞻远瞩地提出调查和开发利用地热资源，开展海洋地质和矿产勘查工作；组织领导地震预报研究工作，直至生命的最后一刻。

李四光于1958年加入中国共产党，1969年当选为中国共产党第九次全国代表大会代表、第九届中共中央委员会委员。

周恩来总理说：“李四光同志是一面旗帜。”

20世纪30年代末证件照。

1946年在重庆。

1948年在英国海滨城市伯恩茅斯。

1952年4月30日在北京。

1 | 3
2 | 4

1、2、3、4—20世纪50年代做学术报告。

1952年在北京地质学院成立大会上讲话。

1954年为地质部揭牌。

1955年8月在大连白云山庄考察莲花状构造。

1956年在北京地质学院讲地壳运动问题。

1957年春在杭州南山招待所住处门前读书。

1957年春在杭州南山招待所住处门前。

1958年加入中国共产党后，特意在北京西山象鼻子沟住所留影。

20世纪60年代初在地质部办公室。

20世纪60年代在办公室看标本。

20世纪60年代在办公室看标本。

20世纪60年代在办公室看标本。

20世纪60年代在办公室看冰川擦痕标本。

20世纪60年代在办公室阅读地质队的来信。

20世纪60年代做关于地质力学问题的学术报告。

20世纪60年代在办公室学习。

20世纪60年代在办公室看资料。

1963年春在家中庭院里。

1963年春在家中庭院里。

1963年初夏散步后在紫竹院住处大门外白果树下小憩。

1963年夏在家中庭院里。

1963年初夏散步后在紫竹院住处大门外白果树下小憩。

1963年初夏散步后在紫竹院住处大门外白果树下小憩。

1971年3月在办公室进行地热工作安排（这是李四光生前最后一张照片）。

青少年时代
Youth
(1889—1920)

1889年10月26日，李四光出生在湖北省黄冈县回龙山镇下张家湾村的一个贫寒的农村私塾教师家庭。

祖父是蒙古族，叫库里，通晓汉文，曾在村里开设私塾，靠教附近的儿童识字、读书为生。后来和一位汉族妇女结婚，生得一子，取名卓侯，改姓李。李卓侯成年后继承父业，终身从事乡村塾师职业。李四光是李卓侯的次子，取名仲揆，生母姓龚，汉族，是一个朴实的农村妇女。

1894年，小仲揆跟着一位叫陈二爹的老先生启蒙，一年后转到父亲李卓侯执教的私塾念书。

李四光的父亲李卓侯和母亲龚氏在湖北省黄冈县回龙山镇香炉山的家门口。

湖北省黄冈县回龙山镇下张家湾村李四光故居。

他勤奋好学，不读死书，遇事爱思考，且心灵手巧。

村东的小山丘旁有一块如小房间般大小的滚圆的巨石，与周围十里八村的石头完全不一样。关于石头的来历，他问遍了村里人都说不清楚。有的老人说，这是天上的陨石。他想：这么大的陨石落下来，怎么没有砸进软软的土里？他把这件怪事一直记在心里。几十年后，他终于找到了答案：原来，这是几十万年前冰川带来的漂砾！

6岁那年，他和父亲外出到长江边上，第一次看见宽阔的长江和江面上来往的船只，他被震撼了。江面上有舢板、帆船，还有几层楼高的大轮船，轮船上面喷吐着黑烟，嗵嗵嗵地响着，拖着长长的白色浪花，比别的船走得都快。父亲告诉他，这是洋人造的火轮船。不需要摇橹，也不需要张帆，轮船里面有烧煤的机器，船靠机器的力量前进。

父亲还告诉他，洋人不仅造火轮船，还造军舰，日本就是靠军舰在甲午战争中打赢了我们，不仅强占了我国台湾，还要我国赔给他们许多银子，什么时候我们有了自己的轮船和军舰，才不会被洋人欺负。仲揆把父亲的话牢记在心里，并立下志愿：将来一定要为国家造出自己的轮船！

小仲揆还特别善良厚道，富有同情心，总是尽可能地帮助有困难的人。9岁那年一个寒冷的冬夜，村里一位老妪的房子失火，他奋不顾身地救火。火灭后，看到老妪衣衫单薄，直打哆嗦，他顾不得自己的伤痛和疲劳，忙请母亲找出一件棉衣送给了老人。

1902年5月，湖广总督张之洞在武昌兴办新学堂。这一年的冬天，仲揆考入武昌第二高等小学堂（又称西路高等小学堂）。由于在填写报名单时，误将姓名栏当成年龄栏，他写了一个“十四”，发现错误后，便在“十”字上加几笔改成“李”字，但觉得“李四”这个名字难免要被人讥笑，正踌躇间，抬头看到中堂上有一块“光被四表”的匾，他灵机一动，在“李四”后面加了一个“光”字。从此以后，“四光”成了名字，“仲揆”成了字。

1904年7月，李四光由官费派往日本留学。到东京后，先入弘文学院普通科学习日本语言文字和初等数理化。三年后，以优异的成绩考入大阪高等工业学校，实现了小时候的愿望，学习造船机械。

李四光在弘文学院学习时，先后结识了宋教仁和马君武。1905年7—8月，李四光同他们一道参加孙中山在东京筹组同盟会的活动。7月30日由孙中山主盟，李四光宣誓加入同盟会，这时，他还不满16岁。孙中山勉励他要“努力向学，蔚为国用”，他牢记孙先生的教导，珍惜每分每秒，刻苦学习。

1910年7月，李四光从大阪高等工业学校毕业，结束了留学日本的七年生活，回到武昌，在湖北中等工业学堂任教。

日本大阪高等工业学校。

日本大阪高等工业学校师生合影。第五排左二是李四光。

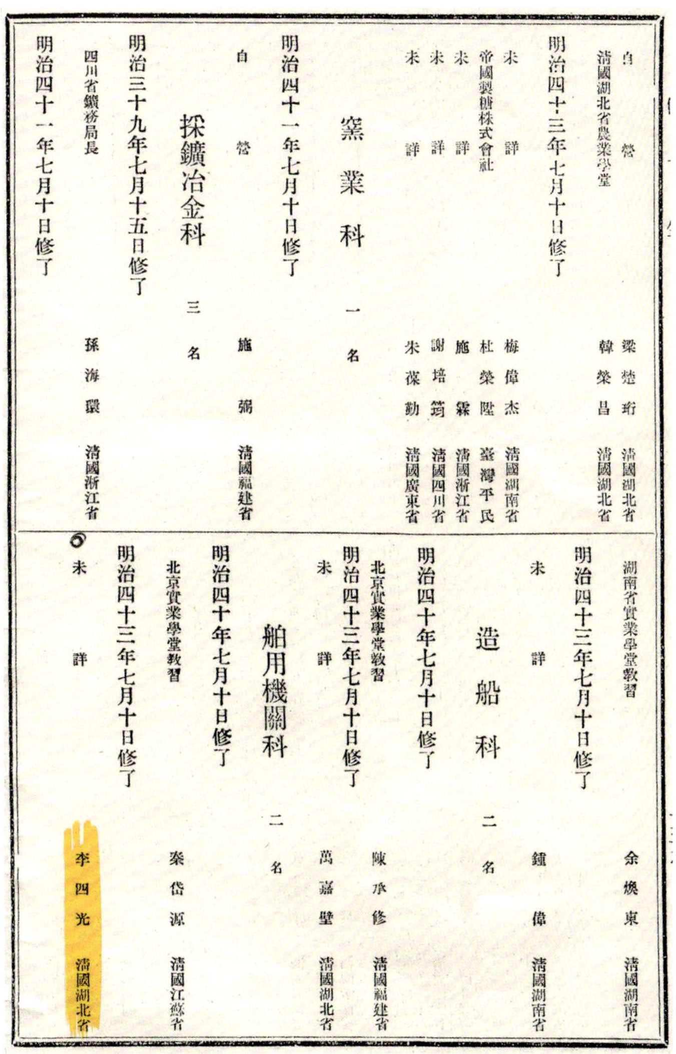

自營　梁燧珩　清國湖北省
清國湖北省農業學堂　韓榮昌　清國湖北省
明治四十三年七月十日修了
未詳　梅偉杰　清國湖南省
帝國製糖株式會社　杜榮陞　臺灣平民
未詳　施霖　清國浙江省
未詳　謝培筠　清國四川省
未詳　朱葆勳　清國廣東省

窯業科　一名

明治四十一年七月十日修了
自營　施弼　清國福建省

採鑛冶金科　三名

明治三十九年七月十五日修了
四川省鑛務局長　孫海環　清國浙江省
明治四十一年七月十日修了

湖南省實業學堂敎習　余煥東　清國湖南省
明治四十三年七月十日修了
未詳　鍾偉　清國湖南省

造船科　二名

明治四十年七月十日修了
北京實業學堂敎習　陳承修　清國福建省
明治四十三年七月十日修了
未詳　萬嘉璧　清國湖北省

船用機關科　二名

明治四十年七月十日修了
北京實業學堂敎習　秦岱源　清國江蘇省
明治四十三年七月十日修了
未詳　李四光　清國湖北省

清政府派出日本的留学生名单。

1911年9月，按照清政府学部的规定，李四光到北京参加辛亥第六次留学毕业生考试。10月成绩公布，他的成绩为“最优等”，被授予“工科进士”。

10月10日，武昌起义爆发。李四光立即离开北京南下，他被委任为湖北军政府理财部参议，参加了革命斗争。

1912年1月1日，南京临时政府成立，孙中山就任临时大总统，正式改国号为“中华民国”，宣告了两千多年的封建帝制在中国历史上的终结。不久，李四光被委任为南京临时政府特派汉口建筑筹备员。湖北同盟会重新建立支部，选举石瑛为支部长，李四光为书记。

2月，湖北军政府设立实业部，李四光被推选为实业部部长。随后，根据南京临时政府内务部的指示，湖北实业部改为实业司，李四光担任司长。

3月，袁世凯篡夺了辛亥革命果实，在北京就任临时大总统。

4月，孙中山辞去临时大总统职务后来到武昌，李四光参加了湖北省军政界召开的欢迎孙中山大会。会后前去探望孙中山。

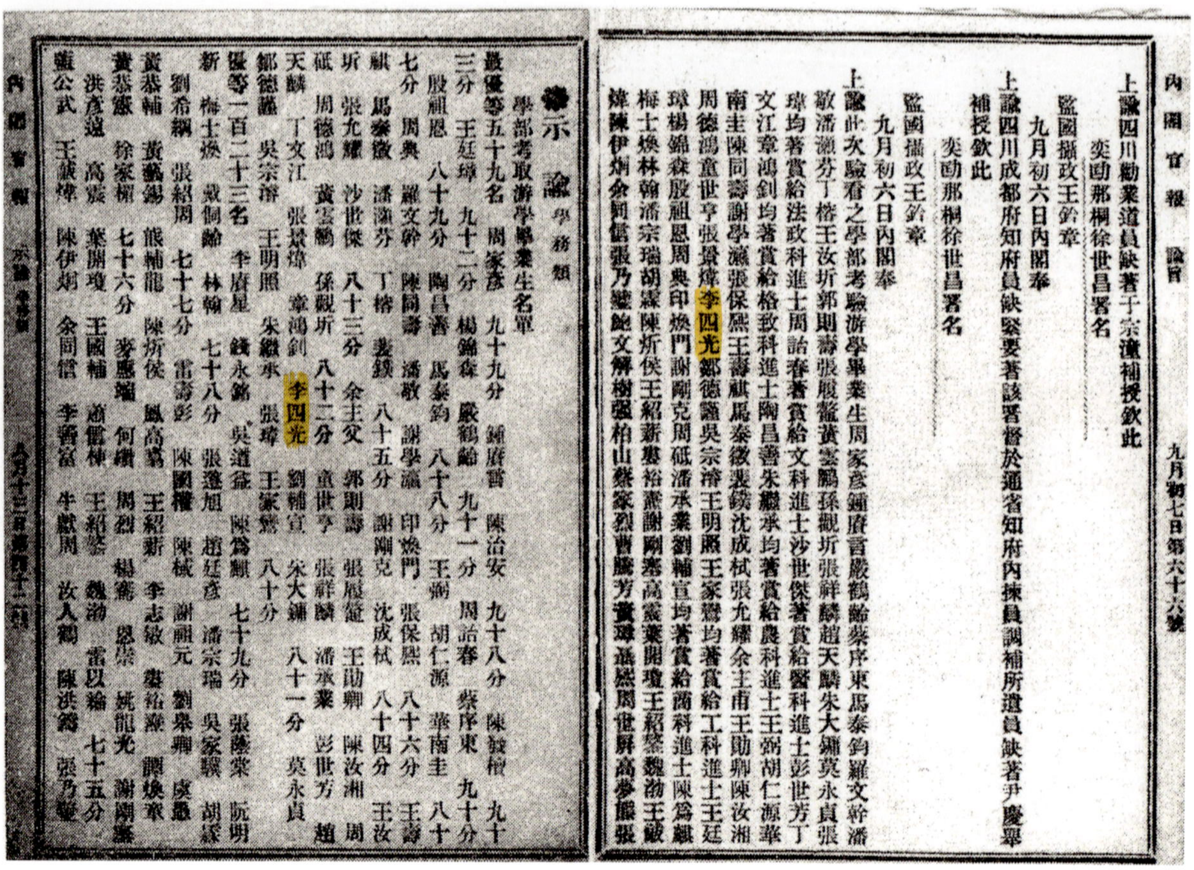

內閣官報 諭旨 九月初七日第六十六號

上諭四川勸業道員缺著于宗潼補授欽此
奕劻那桐徐世昌署名
監國攝政王鈐章
九月初六日內閣奉
上諭四川成都府知府員缺緊要著該署督於通省知府內揀員調補所遺員缺著尹慶舉補授欽此
奕劻那桐徐世昌署名
監國攝政王鈐章
九月初六日內閣奉
上諭此次驗看之學部考驗游學畢業生周家彥鍾賡言嚴鶴齡蔡序東馬泰鈞羅文榦潘敬潘灝芬丁榕王汝圻郭則壽張履鰲黃雲鵬孫觀圻張祥麟趙天麟朱大鏞莫永貞張瑋均著賞給法政科進士周詒春著賞給文科進士沙世傑著賞給醫科進士彭世芳丁文江章鴻釗均著賞給格致科進士陶昌善朱繼承均著賞給農科進士王弼胡仁源華南圭陳同壽謝學瀛張保熙王壽祺馬泰徵裘鋆沈成栻張允耀余主甫王勛鄭陳汝湘周德鴻童世亨張景煒李四光鄒德鑑吳宗濂王明照王家鬱均著賞給工科進士王廷璋楊錦森殷祖恩周典印煥門謝剛克周砥潘承業劉輔宜均著賞給商科進士陳爲麒梅士煥林翰潘宗瑞胡霖陳炘侯王紹薪裘裕蕭謝剛寒高震業開瓊王紹築魏渤王敵煒陳伊炯余同僖張乃鏗饒文解樹强柏山蔡家烈曹驥芳黃璇孫繼周世屏高夢熊張

清宣统三年（1911年）九月内阁官报载李四光经考试通过获“工科进士”。

1912年4月7日孙中山应黎元洪邀请来武汉与湖北军政界人员在都督府合影。第三排右二是李四光。

7月，因不满军阀政府的腐败，李四光以“鄂中财政奇绌，辦（办）事棘手”为理由，愤然辞去实业司司长职务。这时，李四光内心非常郁闷，想到现在既然“力量不够，造反不成”，“不如再读书十年，准备一份力量”，遂向当局提出继续出国留学的要求。

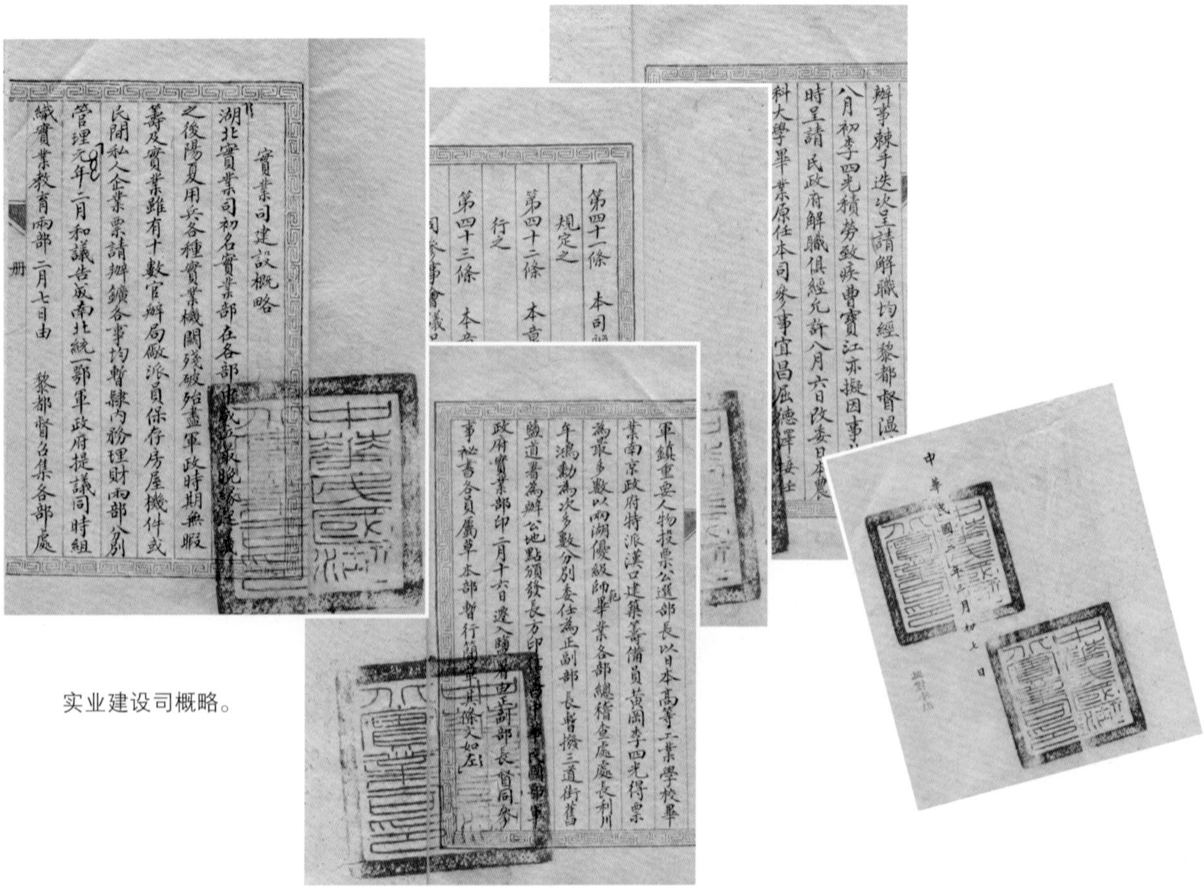
實業司建設概略

湖北實業司初名實業部在各部

之後陽夏用兵各種實業機關殘破殆盡軍政時期無暇

籌及實業雖有十數官辦局廠派員保存房屋機件或

民間私人企業稟請辦鑛各事均暫隸內務理財兩部分別

管理元年二月和議告成南北統一鄂軍政府提議同時組

織實業教育兩部二月七日由　黎都督召集各部處

軍鎮重要人物投票公選部長以日本高等工業學校畢

業南京政府特派漢口建築籌備員黃岡李四光得票

為最多數以兩湖優級師範畢業各部總稽查處處長利川

年鴻勳為次多數分別委任為正副部長

辦事棘手迭次呈請解職均經黎都督

八月初李四光積勞致疾

時呈請　民政府解職俱經允許八月六日改委日本

科大學畢業原任本司參事

实业建设司概略。

1913年7月，李四光在获得临时稽勋局报准后，由上海启程赴欧洲，准备在英国学习采矿。10月，入英国伯明翰大学，先进预科学习。1915年，由采矿系转到地质系，准备从基础学起。

1914年8月，英国对德国宣战，第一次世界大战爆发。由于日用品短缺，物价上涨，李四光利用假期，跑到矿山，找些临时工作，赚点生活费，继续自己的学业。

1917年7月，李四光通过了学士考试。随后，他在鲍尔敦（Bolton）教授指导下，广泛收集当时能收集到的有关中国地质的科学文献，进行仔细阅读，提出自己的评价和见解，于1918年5月用英文写成题为《中国之地质》的论文，提交伯明翰大学地质系。6月通过答辩，被授予自然科学硕士学位。为了在回国之前再多获得一些英国矿山的实地知识，李四光到康卫尔锡矿工作了一段时间。

1919年，旅欧的中国地质调查所所长丁文江找到李四光，建议他回国后到北京大学任教。李四光当时想回国后主要从事地质矿产调查工作，因此准备去欧洲大陆做一次考察后再做决定。

英国伯明翰大学外景。

李四光学习过的教室。

1978年，李四光的老师威尔士（Wills）教授
回忆李四光当年在英国时的情景。

1914年李四光在宿舍中读书。

李四光在英国留学期间，为了调剂紧张的学习生活，特地在旧货市场上买了一把小提琴，请人教他演奏。

1914年李四光（右）在伯明翰大学。

1916年留学期间李四光（右）在矿区打工。

李四光（后排右二）和老师鲍尔敦（后排左一）等郊游留影。

李四光（后排左一）和老师鲍尔敦一家。

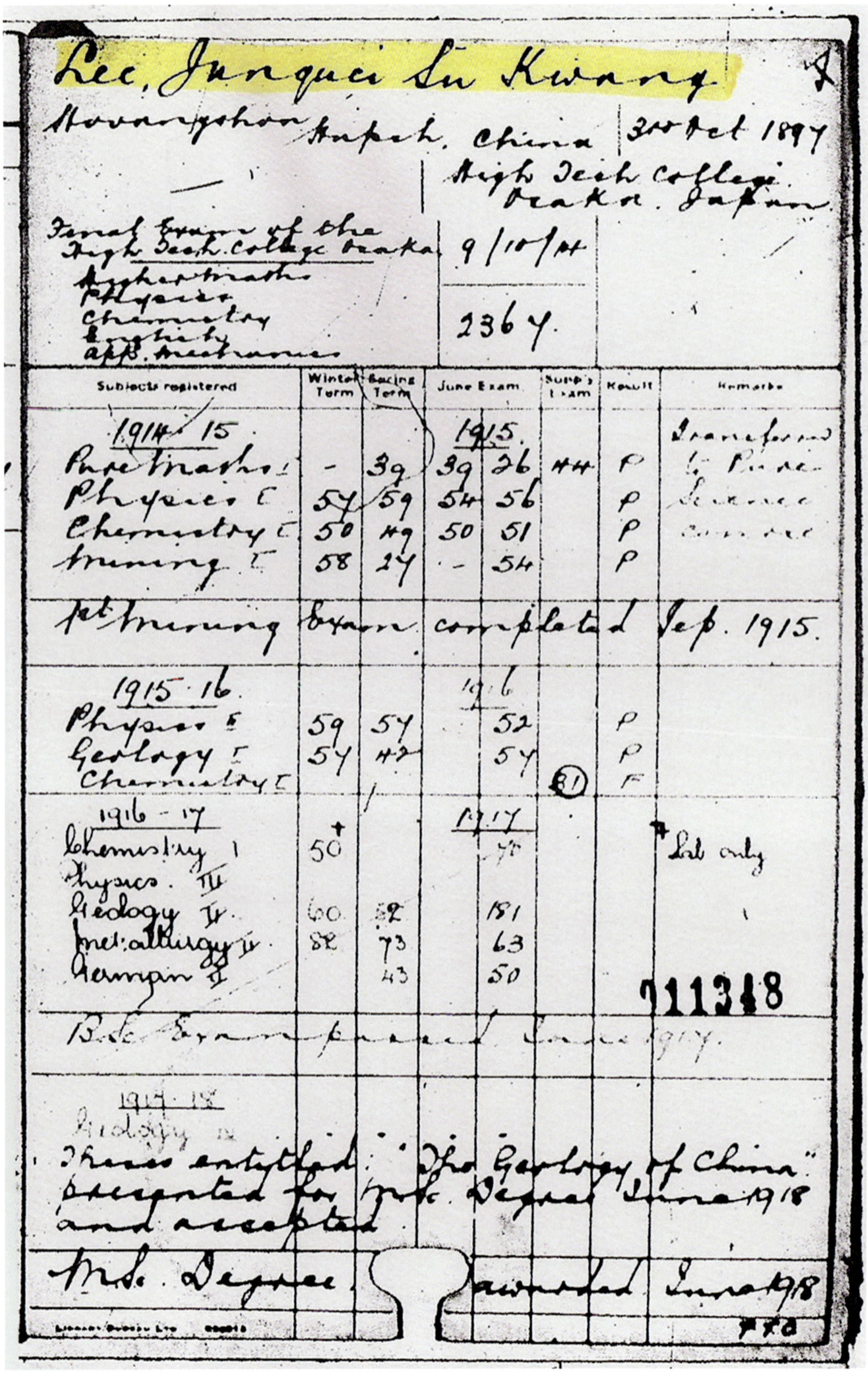

Lee, Jungquei Su Kwang

Hwangchow Hupeh, China | 3rd Oct 1897

High Tech College Osaka, Japan

Final Exam of the High Tech. College Osaka | 9/10/14

Applied Maths, Physics, Chemistry, Electricity, App. Mechanics | 2364

Subjects registered	Winter Term	Spring Term	June Exam		Supp's Exam	Result	Remarks
1914-15			1915.				Transferred to Pure Science course
Pure Maths I	-	39	39	26	44	P	
Physics I	57	59	54	56		P	
Chemistry I	50	49	50	51		P	
Mining I	58	27	-	54		P	
1st Mining Exam completed Sep. 1915.							
1915-16			1916				
Physics II	59	57		52		P	
Geology I	54	42		57		P	
Chemistry I					31	F	
1916-17			1917				
Chemistry I	50*			70			*Lab only
Physics II							
Geology II	60	52		181			
Metallurgy II	82	73		63			
Mining II		43		50			

011348

B.Sc. Exam passed June 1917.

1917-18

Geology III

Thesis entitled: "The Geology of China" presented for M.Sc. Degree June 1918 and accepted

M.Sc. Degree awarded June 1918

李四光在伯明翰大学的学生注册卡。

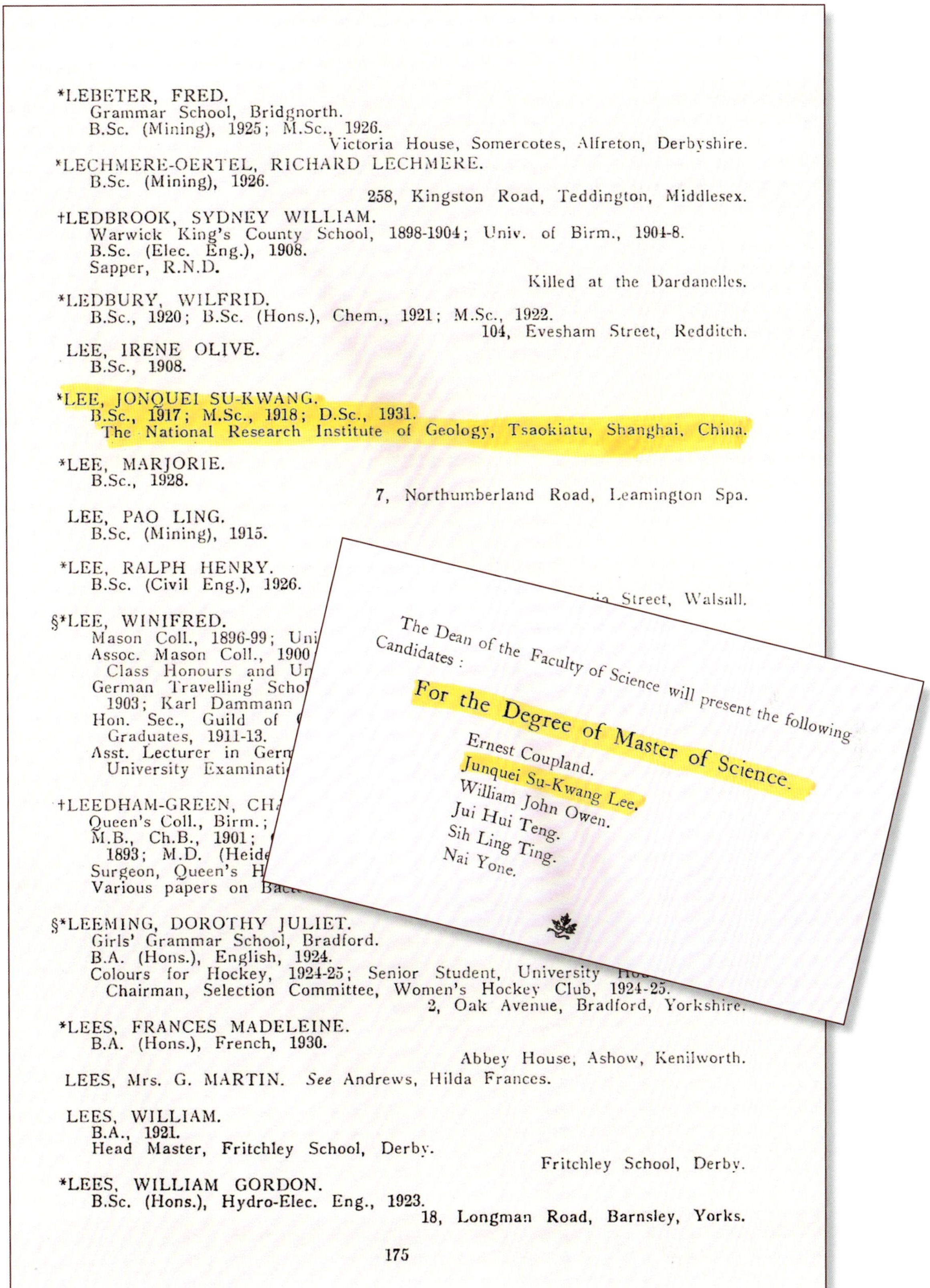

*LEBETER, FRED.
Grammar School, Bridgnorth.
B.Sc. (Mining), 1925; M.Sc., 1926.
Victoria House, Somercotes, Alfreton, Derbyshire.

*LECHMERE-OERTEL, RICHARD LECHMERE.
B.Sc. (Mining), 1926.
258, Kingston Road, Teddington, Middlesex.

†LEDBROOK, SYDNEY WILLIAM.
Warwick King's County School, 1898-1904; Univ. of Birm., 1904-8.
B.Sc. (Elec. Eng.), 1908.
Sapper, R.N.D.
Killed at the Dardanelles.

*LEDBURY, WILFRID.
B.Sc., 1920; B.Sc. (Hons.), Chem., 1921; M.Sc., 1922.
104, Evesham Street, Redditch.

LEE, IRENE OLIVE.
B.Sc., 1908.

*LEE, JONQUEI SU-KWANG.
B.Sc., 1917; M.Sc., 1918; D.Sc., 1931.
The National Research Institute of Geology, Tsaokiatu, Shanghai, China.

*LEE, MARJORIE.
B.Sc., 1928.
7, Northumberland Road, Leamington Spa.

LEE, PAO LING.
B.Sc. (Mining), 1915.

*LEE, RALPH HENRY.
B.Sc. (Civil Eng.), 1926.
...ia Street, Walsall.

§*LEE, WINIFRED.
Mason Coll., 1896-99; Uni...
Assoc. Mason Coll., 1900...
Class Honours and Ur...
German Travelling Scho...
1903; Karl Dammann ...
Hon. Sec., Guild of ...
Graduates, 1911-13.
Asst. Lecturer in Germ...
University Examinati...

†LEEDHAM-GREEN, CHA...
Queen's Coll., Birm.; ...
M.B., Ch.B., 1901; ...
1893; M.D. (Heide...
Surgeon, Queen's H...
Various papers on Bac...

§*LEEMING, DOROTHY JULIET.
Girls' Grammar School, Bradford.
B.A. (Hons.), English, 1924.
Colours for Hockey, 1924-25; Senior Student, University Ho...
Chairman, Selection Committee, Women's Hockey Club, 1924-25.
2, Oak Avenue, Bradford, Yorkshire.

*LEES, FRANCES MADELEINE.
B.A. (Hons.), French, 1930.
Abbey House, Ashow, Kenilworth.

LEES, Mrs. G. MARTIN. *See* Andrews, Hilda Frances.

LEES, WILLIAM.
B.A., 1921.
Head Master, Fritchley School, Derby.
Fritchley School, Derby.

*LEES, WILLIAM GORDON.
B.Sc. (Hons.), Hydro-Elec. Eng., 1923.
18, Longman Road, Barnsley, Yorks.

175

The Dean of the Faculty of Science will present the following Candidates :

For the Degree of Master of Science.

Ernest Coupland.
Junquei Su-Kwang Lee.
William John Owen.
Jui Hui Teng.
Sih Ling Ting.
Nai Yone.

李四光从伯明翰大学获科学硕士的文档。

1920年初，李四光离开英国先到法国巴黎。2月，他应留法勤工俭学会的邀请，做了《现代繁华与炭》的演讲。在开场白中，李四光首先谈到对事物的认识，应该有科学的态度。认为“真正讲学的精神，可以用一句话概括，那就是为真理奋斗”。接着，他根据这几年学习地质的体会，对造成西方繁华的物质基础，谈了自己的看法。认为现代的繁华是与热动力资源特别是煤炭还有“煤油”（指石油）的挖掘分不开的，但是有朝一日这些资源是要烧尽的，那时有什么东西、用什么方法来代替煤炭，维持人类的繁华？为此，他指出了研究解决这个重大问题的各种途径，包括天体转动的、原子裂变的、太阳送来的以及蕴藏于地中的热，等等。

离开法国之后，李四光来到瑞士，登上了阿尔卑斯山，琳琅瑰丽的冰川地貌给他留下了深刻的印象。随后，他转到德国考察。在柏林，他接到从伦敦转来的北京大学校长蔡元培邀请他到北京大学任教的电报。于是他决定回国赴北京大学任教。

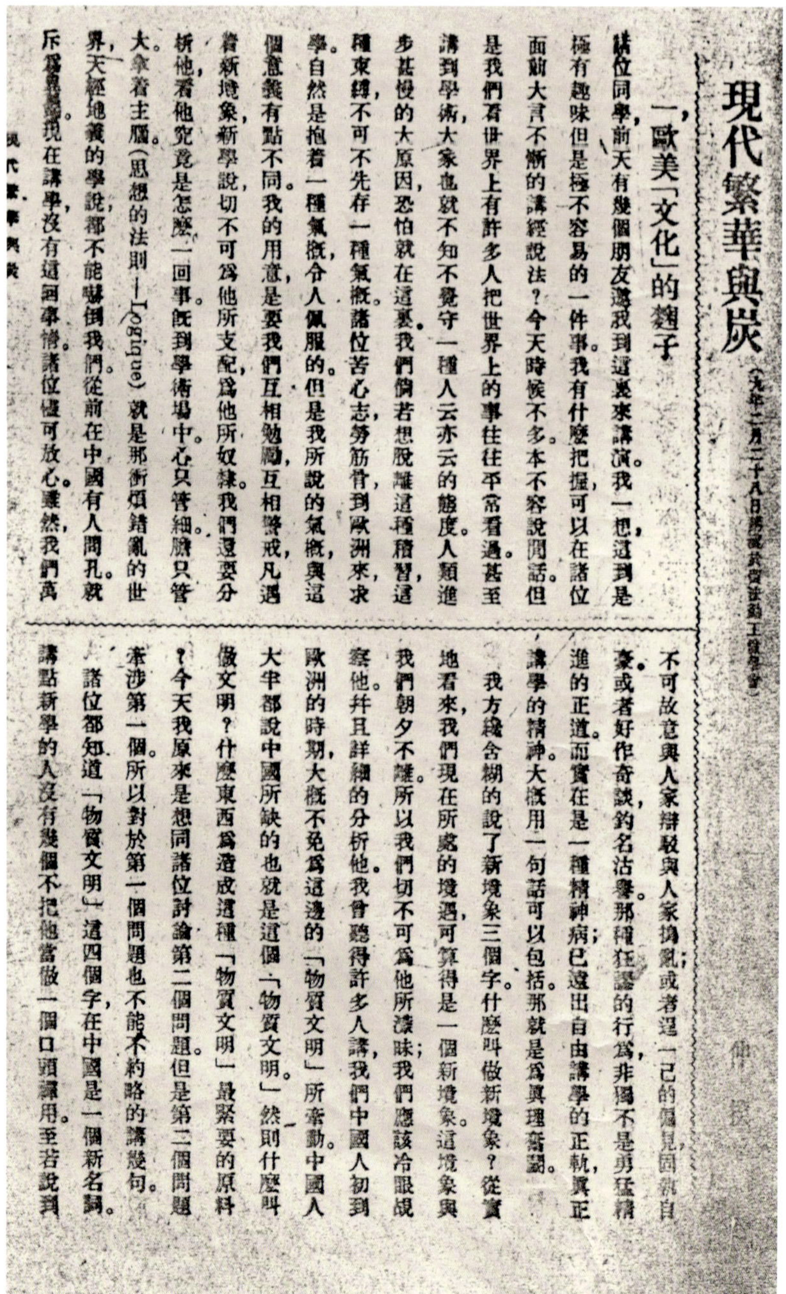

現代繁華與炭

（九年二月二十八日[illegible]留法勤工儉學會）

仲揆

一，歐美「文化」的麴子

諸位同學，前天有幾個朋友邀我到這裏來講演。我一想，這到是一極有趣味，但是極不容易的一件事。我有什麼把握，可以在諸位面前大言不慚的講經說法？今天時候不多，本不容說閒話。但是我們看世界上有許多人把世界上的事往往平常看過。甚至講到學術，大家也就不知不覺守一種人云亦云的態度。人類進步甚慢的大原因，恐怕就在這裏。我們倘若想脫離這種積習，這種束縛，不可不先存一種氣概。諸位苦心志，勞筋骨，到歐洲來，求學。自然是抱着一種氣概，令人佩服的。但是我所說的氣概，與這個意義有點不同。我的用意，是要我們互相勉勵，互相警戒，凡遇着新境象，新學說，切不可為他所支配，為他所奴隸。我們還要分析他，看他究竟是怎麼一回事。既到學術場中，心只管細，膽只管大。拿着主腦。(思想的法則——Logique) 就是那衡煩錯亂的世界，天經地義的學說，都不能嚇倒我們。從前在中國有人問孔，就斥為異端。現在講學，沒有這回事情。諸位儘可放心。雖然，我們萬不可故意與人家辯駁，與人家搗亂；或者逞一己的偏見，固執自豪；或者好作奇談，釣名沽譽。那種狂謬的行為，非獨不是勇猛精進的正道，而實在是一種精神病；已遠出自由講學的正軌。真正講學的精神，大概用一句話可以包括。那就是為真理奮鬪。

我方纔含糊的說了新境象三個字。什麼叫做新境象？從實地看來，我們現在所處的境遇，可算得是一個新境象。這境象與我們朝夕不離。所以我們切不可為他所濛昧；我們應該冷眼觀察他。并且詳細的分析他。我曾聽得許多人講，我們中國人初到歐洲的時期，大概不免為這邊的「物質文明」所牽動。中國人大半都說中國所缺的也就是這個「物質文明」。然則什麼叫做文明？什麼東西為造成這種「物質文明」最緊要的原料？今天我原來是想同諸位討論第二個問題。但是第二個問題牽涉第一個。所以對於第一個問題也不能不約略的講幾句。

諸位都知道「物質文明」這四個字，在中國是一個新名詞。講點新學的人沒有幾個不把他當做一個口頭譯用。至若說到

1920年2月28日李四光在巴黎留法勤工俭学会所做的《现代繁华与炭》之讲演稿。

投身科学事业

Devoted to Science

(1920—1927)

1920年秋，李四光从欧洲回到阔别七年的祖国。1921年1月，他到北京大学地质学系就职，讲授岩石学、高等岩石学、地质测量和地质构造学等课程，开始了他的教授生活。

李四光一面教书，一面进行科学研究。他把备课、讲课，带学生到野外实习，当作不断积累资料、不断思考和研究问题的极好机会。

北京大学任教期间留影。

我国的北部是煤炭资源十分丰富的地区。为了实地了解这些资源分布的情况，李四光带领地质学系学生，先后到河北、山西、河南、山东等地区进行煤田地质调查。通过实地工作，他感到含煤地层的划分，是个重要的问题。而要解决这一问题，就必须首先研究保存在地层（主要是石炭-二叠纪地层）中的微体古生物䗴科的演变历史。从此，我国科学工作者开始了对这类古生物化石的系统研究。1927年，李四光的第一部科学专著《中国北部之䗴科》由中国地质调查所正式出版。为此，他被英国伯明翰大学授予科学博士学位。

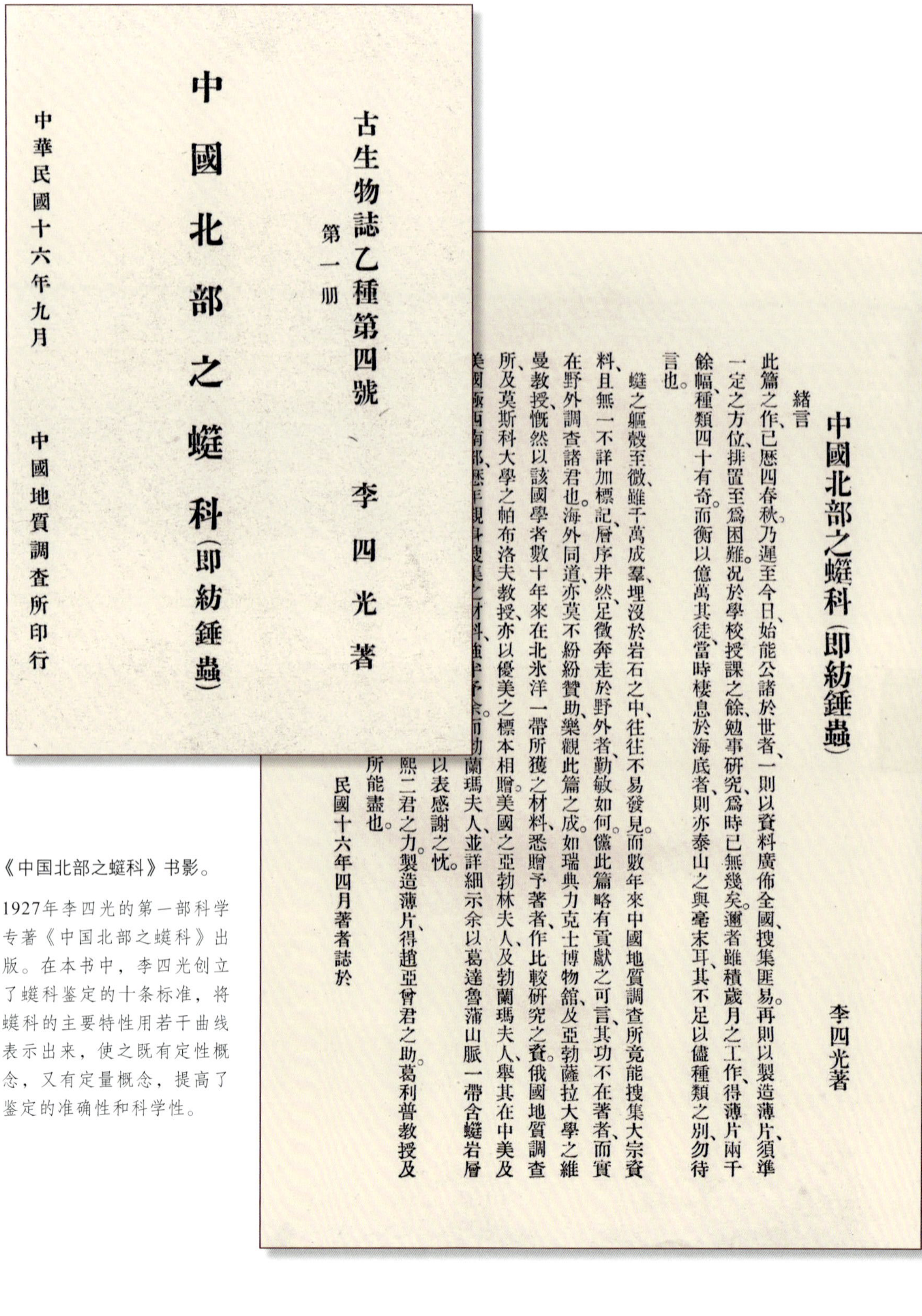

古生物誌乙種第四號 第一冊

李四光著

中國北部之䗴科(即紡錘蟲)

中華民國十六年九月

中國地質調查所印行

中國北部之䗴科(即紡錘蟲)

李四光著

緒言

此篇之作、已歷四春秋、乃遲至今日、始能公諸於世者、一則以資料廣佈全國、搜集匪易、再則以製造薄片、須準一定之方位、排置至爲困難。況於學校授課之餘、勉事研究、爲時已無幾矣、邇者雖積歲月之工作、得薄片兩千餘幅、種類四十有奇、而衡以億萬其徒、當時棲息於海底者、則亦泰山之與毫末耳、其不足以儘種類之別、勿待言也。

䗴之軀殼至微、雖千萬成羣、埋沒於岩石之中、往往不易發見、而數年來中國地質調查所竟能搜集大宗資料、且無一不詳加標記、層序井然、足徵奔走於野外者、勤敏如何、儻此篇略有貢獻之可言、其功不在著者、而實在野外調查諸君也。海外同道、亦莫不紛紛贊助、樂觀此篇之成。如瑞典力克士博物館、及亞勃薩拉大學之維曼教授、慨然以該國學者數十年來在北氷洋一帶所獲之材料、悉贈予著者、作比較研究之資、俄國地質調查所及莫斯科大學之帕布洛夫教授、亦以優美之標本相贈、美國之亞勃林夫人及勃蘭瑪夫人、舉其在中美及美國西南部、歷年親身搜集之材料、盡予余、而勃蘭瑪夫人、並詳細示余以葛達魯蒲山脈一帶含䗴岩層……以表感謝之忱。

……熙二君之力、製造薄片、得趙亞曾君之助、葛利普教授及……所能盡也。

民國十六年四月著者誌於

《中国北部之䗴科》书影。

1927年李四光的第一部科学专著《中国北部之䗴科》出版。在本书中，李四光创立了䗴科鉴定的十条标准，将䗴科的主要特性用若干曲线表示出来，使之既有定性概念，又有定量概念，提高了鉴定的准确性和科学性。

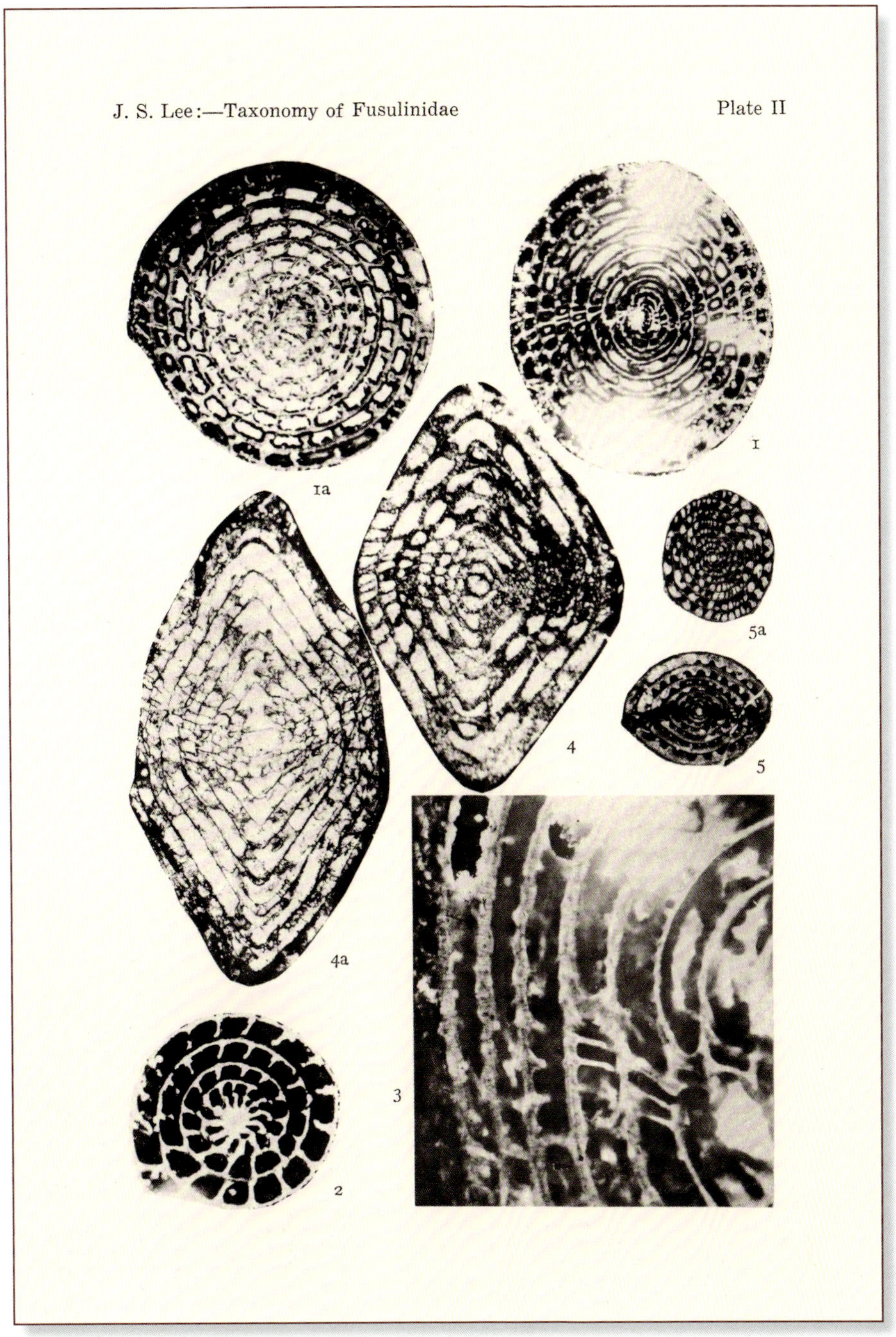

《中国北部之蜓科》图版。

在周口店发掘办事处的院子里合影，左起：裴文中、李四光、德日进、卞美年、杨钟健、巴尔博。

李四光用的照相机。

1921年初夏，李四光（左一）租住在地安门内东吉祥胡同的四合院，与合租的朋友王世杰（左二）、周鲠生（左三）等合影。

李四光在研究石炭-二叠纪地层问题的同时，又先后前往河北省沙河县（今沙河市）和山西省大同盆地，首次发现了第四纪冰川遗迹。他把这两次观察到的现象，用英文写了一篇报道，题为《华北挽近冰川作用的遗迹》，于1922年在美国《地质杂志》上发表，打破了中国近代冰川研究方面的沉寂局面，也为我国第四纪地质的研究揭开了新的一页。这年的1月，中国地质学会召开成立大会，选举章鸿钊为中国地质学会会长，李四光、翁文灏为副会长。

李四光在研究石炭-二叠纪地层过程中，还发现我国北方的石炭-二叠纪地层，主要是由陆相地层构成；而南方的石炭-二叠纪地层，则是海相地层占优势。为什么同一地质时代，海进、海退南北竟有这么大的差异？他认为，这是一个不可忽视的有关地壳运动的重大地质理论问题，需要进行一系列的研究工作。到了1926年5月，李四光在中国地质学会第四次年会上，做了《地球表面形象变迁之主因》的演讲。他在演讲中，依据地球这个旋转体的力学分析和计算，运用当时掌握的若干地质事实，依据海水进退规律研究了地壳运动的方向和起源，为以后地质学的一门新的学说——地质力学的诞生打下了初步基础，也使他成为登上国际地质论坛、加入探讨有关重大地质理论问题行列的第一位中国地质学家。

1923年李四光和北京大学地质学系古生物组毕业生合影。
前排左起：孙云铸、李四光、葛利普、何杰、王烈。

1927年李四光与夫人许淑彬的合影。

在北京大学，李四光除从事教学和科研工作外，还积极参加校务活动。当时军阀混战，教职员工的薪俸被一拖数月、积欠不发。1921年5—6月，北京国立专科以上的八个学校的教职员联合组成索薪团，与军阀政府展开索薪斗争。北京大学索薪团分为四组。李四光同李大钊、马寅初等74人，分在第一组。各组依次出发，会同各校索薪团到军阀政府教育部索讨欠薪。但是，没有什么结果。当他们到新华门总统府请愿时，遭到了反动军警的殴打，李大钊头部受伤。李四光对军阀政府的无理行为，十分愤慨；对北方的政局，颇感烦恼。8月，他同丁西林、王世杰一道辞去北京大学教授职务。9月，蔡元培出国筹措资金返校。经蔡元培的劝说，他们撤回了辞呈。随后，蔡元培请李四光担任北京大学预科委员会委员，李四光接受了。

11月，李四光在《北京大学日刊》上发表了《读书与读自然书》一文，实际上是对胡适提倡“读死书”的异议。李四光说：“书是死的，自然是活的。读书是间接的求学，读自然书乃是直接的求学。只知道书不知道自然的人是书呆子。”他把世界上的书籍分作四类：原著、集著、选著和窃著。认为窃著的作者是“拾取一二人的唾余，敷衍成篇，含糊塞责，断章取义”。他称这种作者叫作“书盗”。

1922年11月，李四光被推选为北京大学评议会评议员。经丁文江推荐，兼任国立京师图书馆副馆长。

1923年1月，李四光与北京女子师范大学附属中学教师许淑彬结婚。他们是经北京大学化学系教授丁绪贤、陈淑夫妇介绍后认识的。举行婚礼的那天，蔡元培当了主婚人，北京大学同事以及地质界的丁文江、翁文灏等都来参加，表示祝贺。10月，许淑彬生下女儿，取名熙芝（后更名李林）。

1923年10月，美国知名的进化论学者奥士本教授到北京大学讲学。讲学前，李四光做了引讲。他在扼要地叙述了奥士本的学说和成就之后，对我国现代科学发展缓慢的因素，提出了自己的看法。他认为五四运动以后，知识界的某些现象是消极的，是令人失望的。如“从大喊大叫一变为无声的观察”，“欣赏一些摇摆不定的想法”，“以及满足于对古籍中只言片语的解释”。他说：“这不是一种真正的变革。真正的变革，必须是通过科学研究，不断适应现代思想发展的趋势。”

1923年1月14日，李四光与许淑彬结婚，蔡元培先生是主婚人。

1927年李四光与夫人许淑彬、女儿李熙芝的全家福。

李四光与女儿李熙芝。

1925年9月，李四光应苏联科学院的邀请，代表北京大学前往列宁格勒和莫斯科，参加该院成立200周年纪念大会。会议期间，李四光会见了卡尔宾斯基、巴甫洛夫等著名学者。

1926年7月，广东国民革命军正式出师北伐。1927年4月，李大钊被奉系军阀张作霖杀害。不久，北京9所国立大专学校被合并为京师大学校，由此，北京大学也一度停办了。

1927年，李四光的妹妹赵希贤与妹夫梅远谋结为伉俪。

1927年妹妹赵希贤（左）、妹夫梅远谋（中）结婚时与李四光（右）的合影。

走自己的路

Creative Spirit

(1927—1937)

1927年的冬天，李四光应南京政府中央研究院院长蔡元培的邀请，离开北京南下，主持地质研究所的筹建工作。翌年1月，地质研究所成立，李四光担任所长。从这时起，直到全民族抗日战争爆发，李四光虽然仍被聘为北京大学研究教授，还兼任过地质学系主任，但主要精力已转到领导地质研究所的工作上了。

1928年李四光与北京大学地质学系学生合影。左起：裴文中、李春昱、朱森、李四光、黄汲清、赤懒安彦、杨曾威。

1930年中央研究院成立两周年纪念会上海同人合影。第一排左起第8人是李四光，第11人是蔡元培，中间站立女孩为李四光之女李林。

李四光在中央研究院地质研究所度过了20多个年头。这是一段艰难的岁月。地质研究所初建时，首先遇到的困难是房屋、图书、仪器设备的缺乏。由于国民党政府建都南京，大小机关纷纷成立，公房全被占用，地质研究所只好随中央研究院暂设在上海。在上海也是临时租用民房，所址几经搬迁，不得安定。李四光后来回忆当时的情景时说："隔不了多久，几个人又要扛起'地质研究所'这块招牌，在上海马路上跑来跑去。"1932年9月，地质研究所由上海迁到南京成贤街中央研究院院部办公。经过这样几年的折腾，直到1933年秋，坐落在南京鸡鸣寺路的办公楼建成，地质研究所才算有了正式的所址。为了把地质研究所办成在学术上有权威的机关，李四光除了吸收一批年轻的、有专长的地质学者来所工作外，还聘请所外有贡献的地质学家为本所的兼任研究员或特约研究员。

20世纪30年代初李四光夫妇（左二、左三）与斯行健夫妇（右一、右二）等的合影。

在地质研究所成立之初百事待理的时候，李四光仍然没有放松对地壳运动基本问题的研究。他当时为什么要选择这样一个复杂而艰巨的研究课题？他认为：“地球表面形象之变迁及变迁的原因，世界地质学者讨论已久。无奈问题既大，牵涉之事实甚多，研究之方法不一，结论因之有异。”“我国地质研究已有十数年之历史，所聚成绩，是以补助研究世界问题之资料。”倘若“有学者出而考察此种问题，旁征博引，作一持平之论，则不独与世界以科学上之贡献，亦且争得国际间之荣誉”。1929年，李四光在英国《地质杂志》上发表的《东亚一些构造型式及其对大陆运动问题的意义》一文，就是这个时期他对东亚及其他地方发现的某些大地构造现象组合研究的一次总结。李四光认为，一切构造现象，绝不是孤立存在的，它

在中央研究院时期的李四光。

们经常是成群出现的，只要鉴定出它们之间确有生成联系，那它们就是属于同一个构造体系。特别是，他提出的山字型构造体系的概念，标志着地质力学发展过程中的一个重要阶段。1929年2月，李四光在中国地质学会第六次年会上被推选为会长。

南京地质研究所现貌。

李四光工作过的地质研究所办公楼。

李四光办公楼前。

李四光在中央研究院地质研究所的办公室。

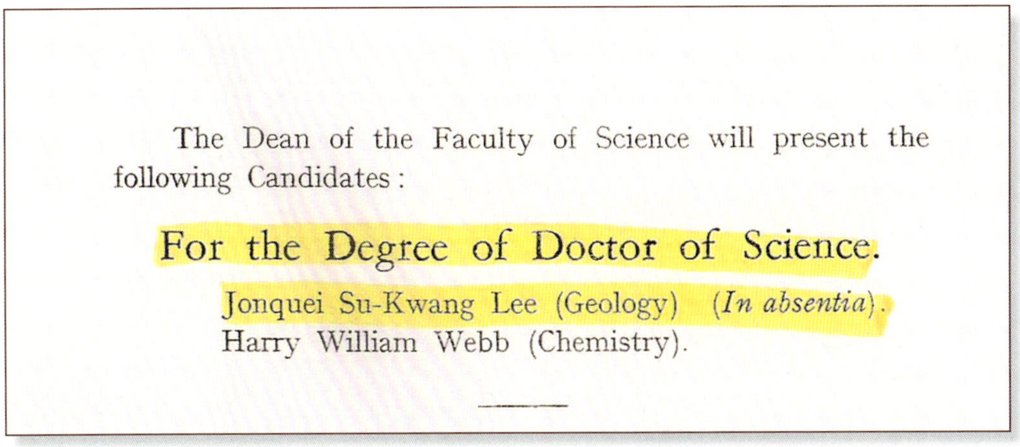

The Dean of the Faculty of Science will present the following Candidates:

For the Degree of Doctor of Science.

Jonquei Su-Kwang Lee (Geology) (*In absentia*).
Harry William Webb (Chemistry).

李四光获科学博士的文档。

1931年李四光的老师鲍尔敦给他来信，告诉他鉴于《中国北部之蜓科》的工作，伯明翰大学决定授予他荣誉科学博士的学位。如果他自己不出席，要请人代领文凭的话，需要花18英镑买一套博士服和帽子穿戴上才能接受文凭。李四光对妻子许淑彬说："我做研究工作不是为名，并且还要花钱，我不想要。我去信感谢他们的好意，同时说明不要这个学位。"妻子许淑彬对他说："人家要之不得，你还不要。不但辜负了你老师的好意，并且失了得科学博士的机会，也是很可惜。"结果妻子自作主张汇去了18英镑，之后接到了学校寄来的文凭。不过这张文凭在逃难到桂林的时候留在了庐山，从此丢失了。

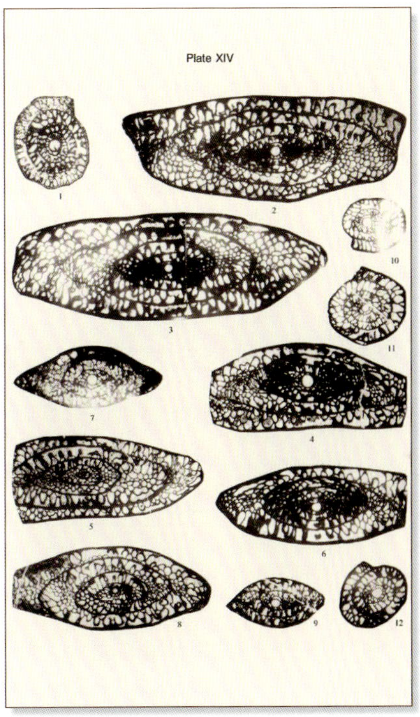

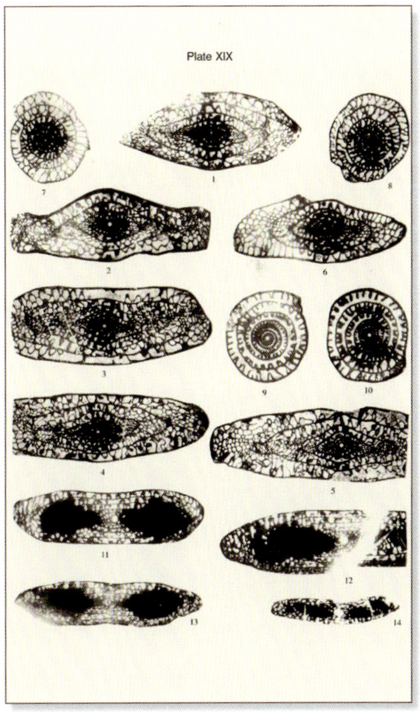

《中国北部之蜓科》图版。

李四光在研究地壳运动问题的同时，并没有放松对第四纪冰川的研究。1930年夏，李四光因病到庐山牯岭休养，感到这里是进行野外地质实习极为合适的地点。第二年，他就带领北京大学地质学系学生到庐山实习。庐山奇特的地质地貌，在李四光心中留下了深思未解的问题。1932年，李四光带着他思考的问题，率领地质研究所的同事，第三次来到庐山。根据勘查所获得的大量资料，李四光把这个夏季看成是“一个幸运的季节”，把庐山称为“困惑难解和耸人听闻学说的诞生场所”，是“中国第四纪冰川的典型地区”。由此，李四光还得出一条非常重要的结论，认为中国第四纪冰川主要是山谷冰川，在有山谷冰川特别发育的山区，才有山麓冰川（即山前冰泛）的发生。这个意见为以后第四纪冰川的研究指明了方向。1933年11月，李四光在中国地质学会第十次年会上，以《扬子江流域之第四纪冰期》为题，做了理事长的学术演讲，详细地论述了庐山地区的第四纪冰川遗迹。

1935年8月李四光在英国《自然》杂志发表题为《中国构造框架》的文章介绍关于地壳运动和大陆车阀的假说。

268 NATURE AUGUST 17, 1935

Tectonic Framework of China

PROF. J. S. LEE delivered a lecture before the Geological Society on June 5 on a subject of which he is the leading authority: "The Structural Pattern of China and its Dynamic Interpretation". Since the time of Suess, it has been generally accepted that the structural framework of eastern Asia consists of a series of arcs with the 'Amphitheatre of Irkusk' as their common centre. Modern researches, however, have shown that each of these arcs embraces features of different tectonic origin. Three main groups of structural elements are now recognised: (*a*) the Cathaysian geosynclines and their complementary geanticlines; (*b*) the east-west zones; and (*c*) the shear-forms. These seem to be fundamentally independent of each other, although they sometimes fall in line and sometimes interfere.

The Palæocathaysian geosyncline existed as an epicontinental trough, more or less parallel with the eastern border of the continent, so far back as late Pre-Cambrian time. A remnant of its borderland still remains in the coastal belt of south-eastern China. Prof. Lee traces its history to Permo-Carboniferous times, when it formed the eastern extension of the Tethys, and on to the Triassic when it formed the Mesocathaysian geosyncline. It was completely filled in during the Lower Jurassic, and since then China has remained continental. Modern features arose from Jurassic-Cretaceous movements and some of them followed the old-established lines, with the result that geosynclines and geanticlines of the Cathaysian type can still be recognised. One of the present-day troughs is occupied by the Sea of Japan and the Yellow Sea; another, farther inland, stretches from the plain of Manchuria to the Central Yangtze Basin and is named the Neocathaysian geosyncline.

The east-west zones, tabulated below, exhibit a rhythmic orogeny that is one of the most striking tectonic phenomena of eastern Asia. It will be noted that the interval between the ranges is 8° of latitude in every case.

The third group of features includes various shear-forms, of which three types predominate. One of these forms consists of a series of nearly parallel folds trending north-east or north-west and is known as the ξ type. These are commonly traversed by faults roughly perpendicular to the axes. Another consists of a frontal arc with a radial backbone, somewhat after the fashion of a bow and arrow, and is called the ε type. The third is a bundle of folds curving round an old massif or mountain mass and is designated the η type.

Orogenic Epochs	Ranges and their latitudes			
	Tannu-Kentai 49°–50°N.	Inshan 41°–42°N.	Tsingling 33°–34°N.	Nanling 25°–26°N.
Tertiary	—	×	?	?
Jurassic-Cretaceous	×	×	×	×
Hercynian	?	?	×	×
Caledonian	×	—	?	×
Pre-Sinian	×	×	×	×

Consideration of the mechanics, supported by experimental reproductions, leads Prof. Lee to the belief that the shear-forms imply horizontal shearing movements of the upper layer of the continental mass, directed on one hand against the Tibetan massif or the shattered ends of the east-and-west ranges, and on the other against the border of the continent. The other features also suggest southerly movement of the continental mass, and it is suggested that the driving force might have been supplied by an i…

Return of Mineral Elements

IT is not generally known that plants can return to the soil at some stage of their growth, either after the first burst of vegetative activity or after maturation of the fruits, certain of the more important nutrient elements which they have absorbed.

Until recently the evidence was meagre, but a series of papers published in Bucharest by Prof. Deleanu and his colleagues[1-3] recording the result of investigations into the function of mineral elements in the life of the plant, has added considerably to our knowledge of this phenomenon.

In 1908 Prof. Deleanu himself[4] found that there was a reversal of the process of absorption of soil constituents, called by him 'negative migration', which occurred in oat plants after they had reached …

… though no actual loss of soil constituents was found. Plants such as the potato, on the other hand, show no such striking change in the rate of absorption …

AUGUST 17, 1935

… recent Bucharest inv… working with wheat, sh… absorption and migration is s… barley, differing only i… of some seventy days in w… three phases: (1) vegetativ… by the twenty-sixth … commences about the t… about the sixty-fifth … Absorption of all min… portions as a whole was r… during phase (1); th… of phosphorus, nitrog… markedly decreased, but no… in the case of potassium… occurred after the first twe… amounts to nearly half th… absorbed more or less regu… some loss of all elements o… the loss was most marked in … calcium, as negative mig… early, but the loss in … than 20 per cent. What … the stage (2) the devel… supplies of nutrients from t… being absorbed directly … supply of nitrogen, phosphoru… inadequate in the leaves and … absorption of these elements … place; potassium and calciu… excess of the amount required … can be returned to the soil.

The phenomenon of negativ… other groups of plants. In t… not only does loss of soil consti… main stem has reached maturi…

… finance of the Institute of … concern, and was the subj… special sub-committee. It …

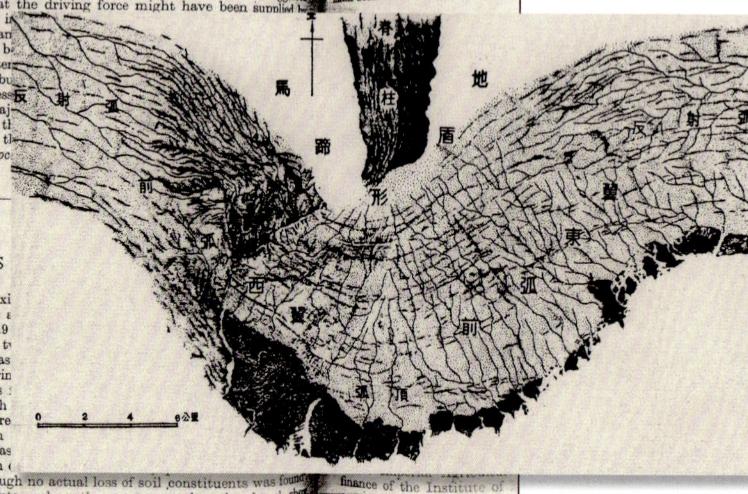

一个小型山字型构造。

李四光在芦林的家。

到了1936年8月，李四光在黄山发现第四纪冰川遗迹之后，又带着助手第四次到庐山考察。1937年，他撰写了《冰期之庐山》这部巨著。后因受时局的影响，搁置了十年未能付印，直到1947年才正式用中英文两种文字同时刊印发行，为我国第四纪冰川地质的研究打开了大门。这一年，挪威奥斯陆大学授予李四光哲学博士学位。

王家坡冰川“U”形谷。

李四光（左）在黄山汤口考察冰川遗迹。

李四光在地质工作中使用的放大镜和罗盘。

李四光在黄山半山寺山谷的山坡石壁上发现的冰川擦痕遗迹。

QUOD FELIX FAUSTUMQUE SIT
COLLEGIUM ACADEMICUM
UNIVERSITATIS OSLOENSIS
EX AUCTORITATE SIBI LEGIBUS DELATA
ET EX DECRETO
ORDINIS MATHEMATICO-PHYSICI
IN VIRUM DOCTISSIMUM
LI SSU KUANG
SUMMOS IN PHILOSOPHIA HONORES
CONFERT
ET
PHILOSOPHIAE DOCTOREM
RITE CREATUM PRONUNCIAT
QUOD HIS LITTERIS
SIGILLO UNIVERSITATIS MUNITIS TESTAMUR
OSLOIAE DIE VII MENSIS MAII ANNI MDCCCCXXXVI
RECTOR UNIVERSITATIS
SECRETARIUS UNIVERSITATIS

奥斯陆大学哲学博士学位证书。

李四光具有强烈的爱国主义思想和刚正不阿的性格。他同情受迫害的人，总想自己能为他们做点什么。1933年春，当李四光得知北京大学师生准备为李大钊举行公葬的消息后，他立即拿出一笔钱送去，表示襄赞这一义举。后来，他还定做了一只大铜墨盒，在盒盖上刻了“铁肩担道义，棘手著文章”作为铭记。6月，当李四光接到蔡元培从上海发来的中央研究院总干事杨铨被特务暗杀的电报后，立即赶到上海，参加商讨善后事宜，并不顾特务

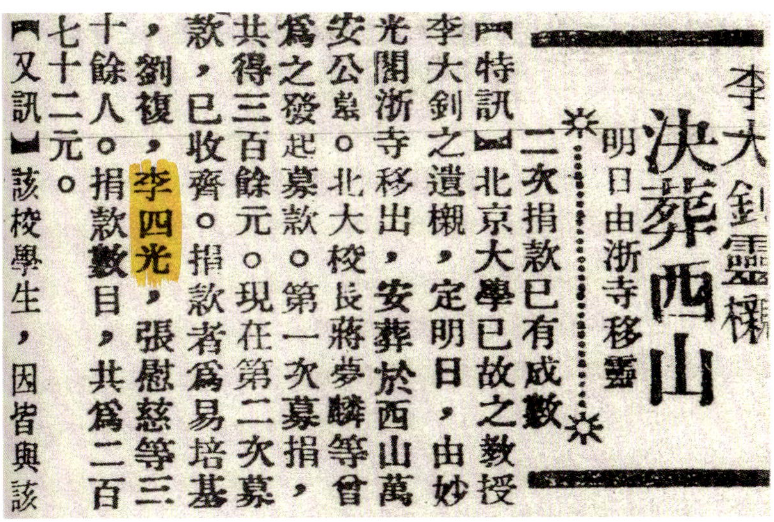
李大釗靈櫬
決葬西山
明日由浙寺移靈
二次捐款已有成數
【特訊】北京大學已故之教授李大釗之遺櫬，定明日，由妙光閣浙寺移出，安葬於西山萬安公墓。北大校長蔣夢麟等曾爲之發起募款。第一次募捐，共得三百餘元。現在第二次募款，已收齊。捐款者爲易培基，劉復，李四光，張慰慈等三十餘人。捐款數目，共爲二百七十二元。
【又訊】該校學生，因省與該

为李大钊公葬捐款。

在英国讲学时的李四光（中央研究院的证件照）。

的监视，参加了送殡仪式。回到南京后，李四光决定把他最近鉴定出来的一个蜓科新属，定名为“杨铨蜓”，用这种科学工作者特有的方式向国民党反动派表示抗议。他写道：“‘杨铨蜓’的命名，是用以纪念中央研究院已故总干事杨铨先生的惨死。凡是为科学事业忠心服务的人，都不能不为这种令人沮丧的境遇而感到痛心。”

1934年12月，根据中英两国交换教授讲学的协议，李四光应邀先后到英国伦敦、剑桥、伯明翰等地的八所大学讲学。他根据多年收集和积累的地质资料，按照自己的观点，写成了具有中国风格的地质学讲义。为了纠正当时西欧一般人总认为西藏不完全是中国的一部分的谬误，他的讲稿的第一章，特意从西藏高原讲起，有意识地把西藏高原列入了中国自然区域的第一位。当然，西藏高原在中国地理上的重要性，也是值得抬高到第一位的。李四光在英国各大学讲学约有半年时间，普遍受到重视和欢迎。讲学结束后，他应英国地质界的请求，决定在英国再住一年，将讲稿整理成书，书名为《中国地质学》，并付印出版。1936年4月，李四光为了考察北美的地质，决定横渡大西洋到美国做一次旅行，然后横渡太平洋回国。

1934年李四光赴英国讲学前在上海拍摄的全家福。

武汉大学老校门。

李四光在赴英讲学前，还应邀到武汉大学去讲学。武汉大学是1928年7月李四光应蔡元培的邀请参加筹建的一所综合性大学。同年8月，他除担任该校筹备委员会委员外，还担任新校舍建筑设备委员会委员长。经过实地勘察，该建筑设备委员会决定，以武昌城外东湖附近珞珈山一带为新校舍地址。第二年，通过了新校舍建筑总设计图、圈定地基、修筑马路等各要案。1932年5月，新校舍落成，李四光与蔡元培等一起参加了典礼。1934年夏末初秋，李四光在武汉大学做了两次学术演讲。一次是讲庐山第四纪冰川遗迹，一次是讲《东亚恐慌中中国煤铁供给问题》。这时，正值日本帝国主义侵占了我国东三省，并大举向华北地区节节进犯的时刻。为此，李四光在第二次演讲时，一开头就痛切万分地说："今天要谈的，不是一般的供给问题，而是中国在日本人侵略之下，中国自身供给煤铁的问题。"他悲愤地说："奉天附近抚顺之烟煤"，"其产量很多，煤质亦佳"，而"目下全区煤田，全在日人势力控制之下矣"。"中国蕴藏之铁矿，为量极少，倘使中国工业发达，全部产量，尚不足供给本国之需要。然而大部分——百分之九十以上——之采取权，完全操诸日人之手。"他大声呼吁："幸国人早日醒悟，急起图之！"这篇演讲，表达了一位爱国的科学工作者，对于国家前途、民族命运的关切和忧虑。

建成后的武汉大学校舍。

1934年夏末秋初，应王世杰邀请李四光在武汉大学做了两次学术讲演。

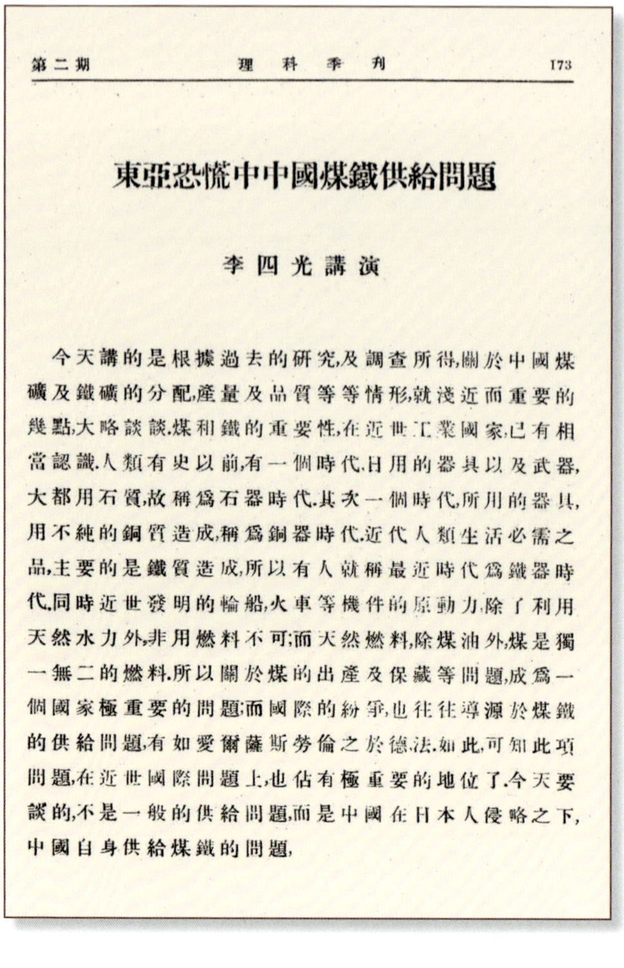

第二期　理科季刊　173

東亞恐慌中中國煤鐵供給問題

李四光講演

今天講的是根據過去的研究,及調查所得,關於中國煤礦及鐵礦的分配,產量及品質等等情形,就淺近而重要的幾點,大略談談.煤和鐵的重要性,在近世工業國家,已有相當認識.人類有史以前,有一個時代,日用的器具以及武器,大都用石質,故稱爲石器時代.其次一個時代,所用的器具,用不純的銅質造成,稱爲銅器時代.近代人類生活必需之品,主要的是鐵質造成,所以有人就稱最近時代爲鐵器時代.同時近世發明的輪船,火車等機件的原動力,除了利用天然水力外,非用燃料不可;而天然燃料,除煤油外,煤是獨一無二的燃料.所以關於煤的出產及保藏等問題,成爲一個國家極重要的問題;而國際的紛爭,也往往導源於煤鐵的供給問題,有如愛爾薩斯勞倫之於德法.如此,可知此項問題,在近世國際問題上,也佔有極重要的地位了.今天要談的,不是一般的供給問題,而是中國在日本人侵略之下,中國自身供給煤鐵的問題,

鄱阳湖，烟波浩渺，湖面宽广。白石嘴，像半岛一样伸向湖中。这里的石灰岩表面有极明显的冰溜条痕，是第四纪冰川的确凿证据之一，十分宝贵，但易受摧残。李四光决定亲自设计，准备在这里盖几间房子，专门陈列冰碛标本。1937年初，“白石陈列馆”快要动工了，国民党的几艘军舰躲进了鄱阳湖，这里成了所谓的“军事要地”。南京国防部限地质研究所人员两天内搬走。虽经多次交涉，但毫无结果。李四光气得一时说不出话来，几天吃不下饭。

全民族抗日战争全面爆发后，蒋介石、汪精卫邀请全国各大学教授及各界领袖分批来庐山谈话，交换对政治、经济、教育等方面的意见。李四光虽然当时身在庐山，却断然拒绝了他们的邀请。

1935年李四光（中）和学生李春昱（左）、王恒升（右）在阿尔卑斯山考察冰川现象。

1935年在伯明翰大学讲学时与友人合影。第三排右一是李四光，站在他身后的是威尔士教授。

Copy of letter from Professor L.J. Wills

I think now will be over 90 years old.

3rd February, 1973

Dear Mr Harland,

Obituary of Jonqui S. Lee

I find that my memory is very vague about dates, Chinese Revolutions and exactly what part Lee played in the years between the 1st Great War and his death. I will try to find out from the University when he arrived at Birmingham It must have been immediately after the war around 1920 when the University building was still occupied by War hospital or just after.

When I first met him he was a bit older than the usual run of students. He has had a very good education, rendering and writing Chinese as taught to the assistants under the Imperial Rule, but he also spoke and wrote perfect English (and I think French), and also was a proficient mathematician (and chemist and physicist I believe). He became a true friend of mine and my family; amongst other things he made for my children a beautiful model monoplane (then a new idea born of the war). He learnt to play the violin, which always struck me as wonderful that since our music and Chinese differ so radically.

He was a Southern Chinese and at first was centred on Nanking but soon moved to P eking after the collapse of Empire. With a few others he helped from a geological survey, and I have a snap of him in the field when a survey party had to have a military guard. He always, I think recognized that this discovery and evaluation of mineral wealth ultimately depends on a 'pure science' foundation. His special field at first was Palaeontology and he described nummulites and their zonal value. I recall that two of his species were Boultonia Rawi and B. Willsi after the three members of our staff at the time. But the megatectonics - mountain ranges and their origin gripped him early. The outcome of these early surveys and of a full knowledge of what had been discovered in other parts of the world resulted in his Geology of China (date?). He came to England to get a publishr, I think it was on that visit that the University awarded him a D.Sc degree on the evidence of the book and other publications (I will try to varify dates). At this time he tried to get experimental evidence for his theory of the drifting of the crust and crumpling of mountain chain arcs (? from the pole equator wards or was it the other way?) as a result of this spin of the earth. He used my Laboratory and the Engineering Department to set up a sphere coated with a thin layer of wax and spin it very rapidly. I think nothing very much happened, and he had to return to China taking the model with him. His last letter to me dated 1965 was 'from' Institute of Geomechanics. He said that "fortunatel I am assigned to a team of young people". Evidently this interest persisted to the end. "I spent most of my time there".

I can't put a date to what follows but I think it must be late 1930's. Lee was the first to discover evidence of Pleistocene Glaciation in China. On a visit to this country he was anxious to see our evidence in a mountainous district and as I was taking a student Field Class at Llangollen, I invited him to join us. He arrived with a small dispatch case stuffed with books, but

- 2 -

in two students in my car to study glacial
when we got there the mist and rain were almost
y Pass. We set out however but before long we
t of the higher levels. I had no map and we lost
n to the Copper mine track and the lake with the
ed at a lake we walked right round it without
was not Llyn Llgdawr.

y made the second lake but every one was soaked,
wn shoes skipped from tussock to tussock - and so
shoes! No complaints, however, but regrets that

he says that evidence glaciations has now been
eas and also outwash forms and it is no longer
untry was glacial but rather how many times!

ar he suffered much from starvation and malnutrition
t. Harry Whittington will be able to fill in some
d possibly you yourself also.

to get to England again about 1947 or 48, but he
saw something of him and his wife and daughter then,
gical interest.

5 I had only one pathetic note if one can call it
e West was dangerous under communist rule. I had
acoge graphical atlas, I think. No acknowledgement
packet of tiny photos of Peking (as sold to
he back of one was "Best wishes J.S. Lee".

out look must have suffered greatly by reason of
llow scientists in the West. He made one trip to Russi

this scrawl. I am getting by with one eye, having
from the other and not yet allowed the special
en freely, hoping that you will be able to use what
You could I expect, get a list of Lee's publications
with dates which might help to date his visits
sely.

Yours sincerely,

L.J. Wills

1973年威尔士教授撰写的追思李四光的文章。

烽火岁月
Conflict Years
(1937—1947)

1937年8月，日本侵略军在上海金山卫登陆之后，出动飞机轮番轰炸南京。地质研究所被南京防空司令部征用，全所暂时迁到了庐山。在这动乱年代，地质研究所迁往哪里？李四光考虑决定迁到当时广西省（今广西壮族自治区）的首府桂林。他之所以做出这样的决定，是因为他意识到，全民族抗日战争全面爆发以后，要长期保守沿海及滨江的重镇，实际上恐难办到，将来长期抗战的根据地实在内地，应该早到内地去做些准备工作。而这时，曾在南京临时政府时期担任过实业部次长的马君武，正在桂林参与创办广西大学。此前他们曾议论过，准备在广西大学内设立一个科学实验馆，招纳技术人才，从事种种战时必需的物资器材的研究。他们的这个意见，得到了李宗仁的赞许。11月，李四光与地质研究所同事一行，乘船溯江西上，途经长沙，向桂林进发。从此，在抗战的艰难岁月里，李四光在桂林度过了将近七个春秋。

1939年由伦敦托马斯－莫尔比公司（Thomas Murby Co.）出版《中国地质学》英文版（*The Geology of China*）；1952年被译成俄文，由苏联莫斯科外文书籍出版局出版；1952年张文佑编译的中文版由南京正风出版社出版。

1938年在广西桂林地质研究所前李四光夫妇和研究所同事合影。第二排中是李四光，第三排中是夫人许淑彬。

李四光到达桂林后不久，接受了广西当局的邀请，担任广西建设研究会的研究员。这个研究会是1937年10月成立的，李宗仁担任会长，白崇禧、黄旭初担任副会长。1939年9月，李四光发表了《建设广西的几个基本问题之商榷》一文。文章指出：中国近年以来，"在各大都会里，洋房马路及其他种种近代物质上的设施，确实增加不少。但是，这一类物质上的建设，对于一般民众究竟有多少利益，却是问题；整个国家民族的力量，因此增加了多少，也不无疑问。""试问上海是什么地方？是外国人到中国来开辟殖民地的登陆点。""北伐成功以后，我们满以为必在内地建立若干重心。一切建设事业，从那些重心向海口推进，直到肿毒消除，我们才有完全独立自主的国家。那知道火上加油……，做错了不说，有人还要曲辩，说迁就既成的事实易收效果。那么，我们何必要革命？又何必要死人牺牲，求一个独立自主的国家？""过去的错误，社会上的人士，尤其是自称有知识的人士，固然不能不负很大的责任，政府呢？"接着，文章从全国的地势，分析了建设广西的重要性。认为："广西虽然没有山西那样大好的煤田，然而在华南的地位，至少从军事上说，不亚于山西。""山西的教训太痛苦了，我们决不能让平型关、雁门关、娘子关的故事重演。""广西防御的设施，决不可以地方建设事业看待，而应该当作整个国防上重大问题，作有效的处置。"这篇文章，表达了一位真诚的爱国者，在全民族抗日战争时期，对国民党政府所作所为不满的心态。

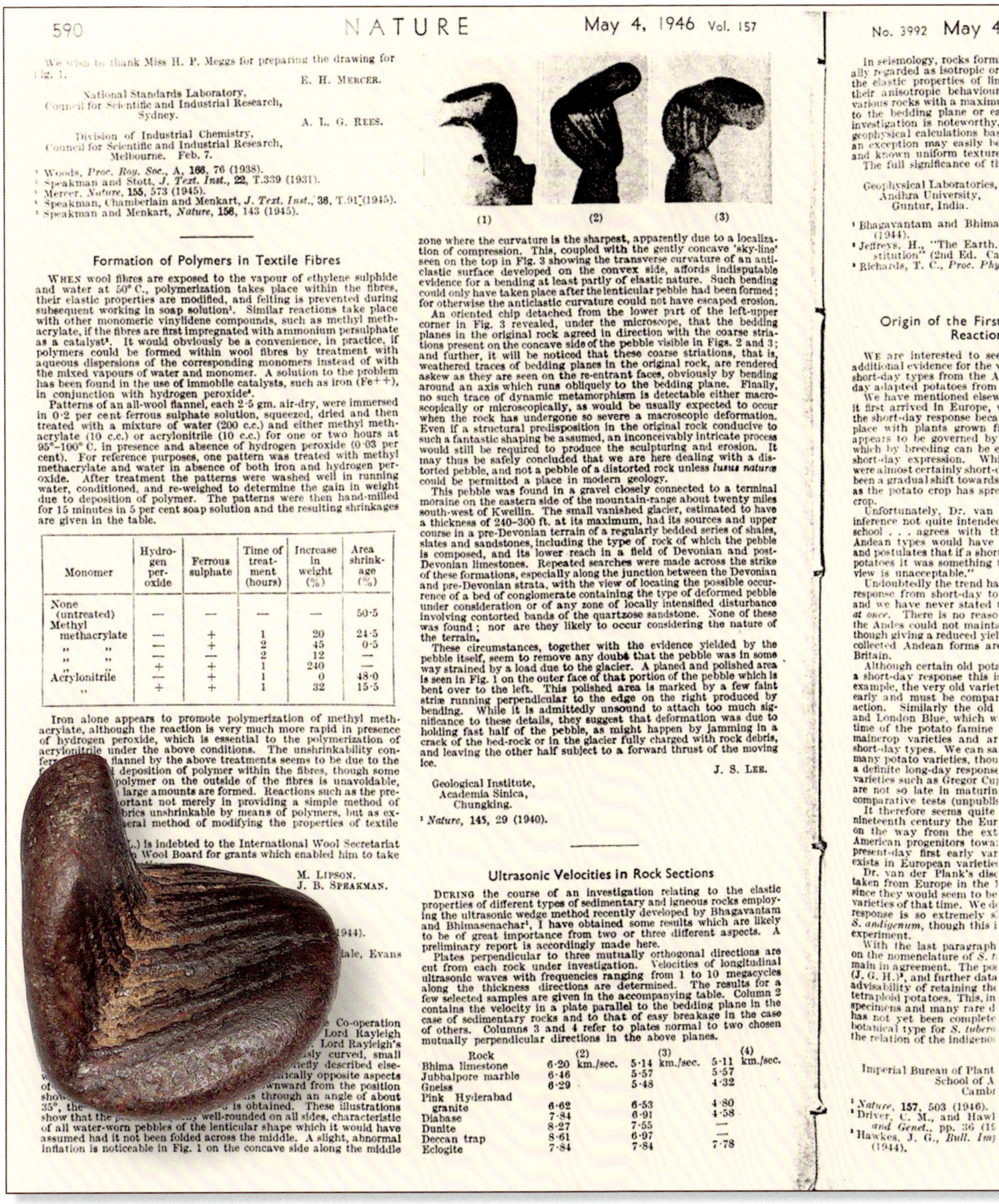

590 NATURE May 4, 1946 Vol. 157

We wish to thank Miss H. P. Meggs for preparing the drawing for Fig. 1.

E. H. MERCER.

National Standards Laboratory,
Council for Scientific and Industrial Research,
Sydney.

A. L. G. REES.

Division of Industrial Chemistry,
Council for Scientific and Industrial Research,
Melbourne. Feb. 7.

[1] Woods, *Proc. Roy. Soc.*, A, **166**, 76 (1938).
[2] Speakman and Stott, *J. Text. Inst.*, **22**, T.339 (1931).
[3] Mercer, *Nature*, **155**, 573 (1945).
[4] Speakman, Chamberlain and Menkart, *J. Text. Inst.*, **36**, T.91 (1945).
[5] Speakman and Menkart, *Nature*, **156**, 143 (1945).

Formation of Polymers in Textile Fibres

WHEN wool fibres are exposed to the vapour of ethylene sulphide and water at 50° C., polymerization takes place within the fibres, their elastic properties are modified, and felting is prevented during subsequent working in soap solution[1]. Similar reactions take place with other monomeric vinylidene compounds, such as methyl methacrylate, if the fibres are first impregnated with ammonium persulphate as a catalyst[2]. It would obviously be a convenience, in practice, if polymers could be formed within wool fibres by treatment with aqueous dispersions of the corresponding monomers instead of with the mixed vapours of water and monomer. A solution to the problem has been found in the use of immobile catalysts, such as iron (Fe^{++}), in conjunction with hydrogen peroxide[3].

Patterns of an all-wool flannel, each 2·5 gm. air-dry, were immersed in 0·2 per cent ferrous sulphate solution, squeezed, dried and then treated with a mixture of water (200 c.c.) and either methyl methacrylate (10 c.c.) or acrylonitrile (10 c.c.) for one or two hours at 95°–100° C. in presence and absence of hydrogen peroxide (0·03 per cent). For reference purposes, one pattern was treated with methyl methacrylate and water in absence of both iron and hydrogen peroxide. After treatment the patterns were washed well in running water, conditioned, and re-weighed to determine the gain in weight due to deposition of polymer. The patterns were then hand-milled for 15 minutes in 5 per cent soap solution and the resulting shrinkages are given in the table.

Monomer	Hydrogen peroxide	Ferrous sulphate	Time of treatment (hours)	Increase in weight (%)	Area shrinkage (%)
None (untreated)	—	—	—	—	50·5
Methyl methacrylate	—	+	1	20	24·5
,, ,,	—	+	2	45	0·5
,, ,,	—	—	2	12	—
,, ,,	+	+	1	240	—
Acrylonitrile	—	+	1	0	48·0
,,	+	+	1	32	15·5

Iron alone appears to promote polymerization of methyl methacrylate, although the reaction is very much more rapid in presence of hydrogen peroxide, which is essential to the polymerization of acrylonitrile under the above conditions. The unshrinkability confer… flannel by the above treatments seems to be due to the … deposition of polymer within the fibres, though some … polymer on the outside of the fibres is unavoidable, … large amounts are formed. Reactions such as the pre… …ortant not merely in providing a simple method of … …brics unshrinkable by means of polymers, but as ex… …eral method of modifying the properties of textile

…L.) is indebted to the International Wool Secretariat … Wool Board for grants which enabled him to take

M. LIPSON.
J. B. SPEAKMAN.

…1944).

…dale, Evans

… Co-operation … Lord Rayleigh … Lord Rayleigh's …usly curved, small …riefly described else… …ically opposite aspects … …wnward from the position … through an angle of about 35°, the … is obtained. These illustrations show that the … well-rounded on all sides, characteristic of all water-worn pebbles of the lenticular shape which it would have assumed had it not been folded across the middle. A slight, abnormal inflation is noticeable in Fig. 1 on the concave side along the middle

(1) (2) (3)

zone where the curvature is the sharpest, apparently due to a localization of compression. This, coupled with the gently concave 'sky-line' seen on the top in Fig. 3 showing the transverse curvature of an anticlastic surface developed on the convex side, affords indisputable evidence for a bending at least partly of elastic nature. Such bending could only have taken place after the lenticular pebble had been formed; for otherwise the anticlastic curvature could not have escaped erosion.

An oriented chip detached from the lower part of the left-upper corner in Fig. 3 revealed, under the microscope, that the bedding planes in the original rock agreed in direction with the coarse striations present on the concave side of the pebble visible in Figs. 2 and 3; and further, it will be noticed that these coarse striations, that is, weathered traces of bedding planes in the original rock, are rendered askew as they are seen on the re-entrant faces, obviously by bending around an axis which runs obliquely to the bedding plane. Finally, no such trace of dynamic metamorphism is detectable either macroscopically or microscopically, as would be usually expected to occur when the rock has undergone so severe a macroscopic deformation. Even if a structural predisposition in the original rock conducive to such a fantastic shaping be assumed, an inconceivably intricate process would still be required to produce the sculpturing and erosion. It may thus be safely concluded that we are here dealing with a distorted pebble, and not a pebble of a distorted rock unless *lusus naturæ* could be permitted a place in modern geology.

This pebble was found in a gravel closely connected to a terminal moraine on the eastern side of the mountain-range about twenty miles south-west of Kweilin. The small vanished glacier, estimated to have a thickness of 240–300 ft. at its maximum, had its sources and upper course in a pre-Devonian terrain of a regularly bedded series of shales, slates and sandstones, including the type of rock of which the pebble is composed, and its lower reach in a field of Devonian and post-Devonian limestones. Repeated searches were made across the strike of these formations, especially along the junction between the Devonian and pre-Devonian strata, with the view of locating the possible occurrence of a bed of conglomerate containing the type of deformed pebble under consideration or of any zone of locally intensified disturbance involving contorted bands of the quartzose sandstone. None of these was found; nor are they likely to occur considering the nature of the terrain.

These circumstances, together with the evidence yielded by the pebble itself, seem to remove any doubt that the pebble was in some way strained by a load due to the glacier. A planed and polished area is seen in Fig. 1 on the outer face of that portion of the pebble which is bent over to the left. This polished area is marked by a few faint striæ running perpendicular to the edge on the right produced by bending. While it is admittedly unsound to attach too much significance to these details, they suggest that deformation was due to holding fast half of the pebble, as might happen by jamming in a crack of the bed-rock or in the glacier fully charged with rock debris, and leaving the other half subject to a forward thrust of the moving ice.

J. S. LEE.

Geological Institute,
Academia Sinica,
Chungking.

[1] *Nature*, 145, 29 (1940).

Ultrasonic Velocities in Rock Sections

DURING the course of an investigation relating to the elastic properties of different types of sedimentary and igneous rocks employing the ultrasonic wedge method recently developed by Bhagavantam and Bhimasenachar[1], I have obtained some results which are likely to be of great importance from two or three different aspects. A preliminary report is accordingly made here.

Plates perpendicular to three mutually orthogonal directions are cut from each rock under investigation. Velocities of longitudinal ultrasonic waves with frequencies ranging from 1 to 10 megacycles along the thickness directions are determined. The results for a few selected samples are given in the accompanying table. Column 2 contains the velocity in a plate parallel to the bedding plane in the case of sedimentary rocks and to that of easy breakage in the case of others. Columns 3 and 4 refer to plates normal to two chosen mutually perpendicular directions in the above planes.

Rock	(2) km./sec.	(3) km./sec.	(4) km./sec.
Bhima limestone	6·20	5·14	5·11
Jubbalpore marble	6·46	5·57	5·57
Gneiss	6·29	5·48	4·32
Pink Hyderabad granite	6·62	6·53	4·80
Diabase	7·84	6·91	4·58
Dunite	8·27	7·55	—
Deccan trap	8·61	6·97	—
Eclogite	7·84	7·84	7·78

No. 3992 May 4

In seismology, rocks formi
ally regarded as isotropic or
the elastic properties of lin
their anisotropic behaviour
various rocks with a maximu
to the bedding plane or ea
investigation is noteworthy,
geophysical calculations bas
an exception may easily be
and known uniform texture
The full significance of th

Geophysical Laboratories,
Andhra University,
Guntur, India.

[1] Bhagavantam and Bhima
(1944).
[2] Jeffreys, H., "The Earth.
stitution" (2nd Ed. Ca
[3] Richards, T. C., *Proc. Phy*

Origin of the First … Reaction

WE are interested to see
additional evidence for the v
short-day types from the A
day adapted potatoes from
We have mentioned elsew
it first arrived in Europe, v
the short-day response beca
place with plants grown fi
appears to be governed by
which by breeding can be e
short-day expression. Whi
were almost certainly short-d
been a gradual shift towards
as the potato crop has spre
crop.
Unfortunately, Dr. van
inference not quite intended
school . . . agrees with th
Andean types would have
and postulates that if a short
potatoes it was something t
view is unacceptable."
Undoubtedly the trend ha
response from short-day to
and we have never stated t
at once. There is no reaso
the Andes could not mainta
though giving a reduced yiel
collected Andean forms are
Britain.
Although certain old pota
a short-day response this is
example, the very old variet
early and must be compar
action. Similarly the old
and London Blue, which w
time of the potato famine
maincrop varieties and ar
short-day types. We can sa
many potato varieties, thou
a definite long-day response
varieties such as Gregor Cu
are not so late in maturin
comparative tests (unpublis
It therefore seems quite
nineteenth century the Eur
on the way from the ext
American progenitors towa
present-day first early var
exists in European varietie
Dr. van der Plank's disc
taken from Europe in the 1
since they would seem to be
varieties of that time. We d
response is so extremely s
S. andigenum, though this i
experiment.
With the last paragraph
on the nomenclature of *S. t*
main in agreement. The po
(J. G. H.)[3], and further data
advisability of retaining the
tetraploid potatoes. This, in
specimens and many rare d
has not yet been complete
botanical type for *S. tubero*
the relation of the indigeno

Imperial Bureau of Plant
School of A
Cambr

[1] *Nature*, **157**, 503 (1946).
[2] Driver, C. M., and Hawk
and Genet., pp. 36 (19
[3] Hawkes, J. G., *Bull. Imp*
(1944).

《一个弯曲的砾石》英文版

这颗变形的砾石是在冰碛层中发现的，它独特的造型引起了李四光的特别注意。他认为变形是由于砾石的一半被固紧，而另一半受到冰流的前推作用形成。砾石的弯曲没有高温作用因素，时间是重要的因素。他将这一发现写成了一篇文章，以《一个弯曲的砾石》为题发表在1946年5月的英国《自然》杂志上。

一次李四光到广西大学做演讲，向听众介绍这颗砾石，称它为极有价值的标本，并拿给听演讲的人传看。结果演讲结束后砾石不见了，李四光后悔不迭，当场反复解释，这颗砾石不是宝石，只是具有科学研究方面的价值。经过一番波折，这颗砾石失而复得。经过这场风波，李四光一直将这颗弯曲的砾石珍藏在身边，不再轻易示人，直到他逝世。

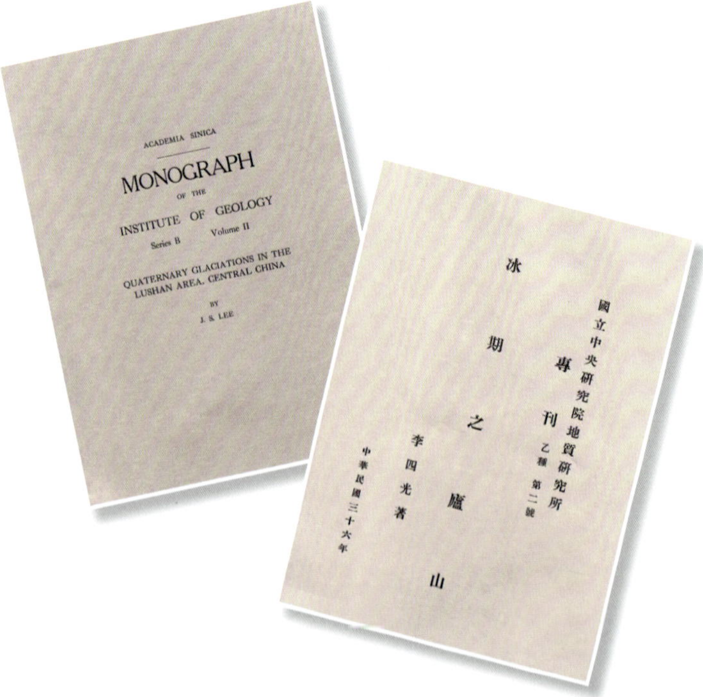

ACADEMIA SINICA

MONOGRAPH OF THE INSTITUTE OF GEOLOGY

Series B Volume II

QUATERNARY GLACIATIONS IN THE LUSHAN AREA, CENTRAL CHINA

BY

J. S. LEE

國立中央研究院地質研究所專刊 乙種 第二號

冰期之廬山

李四光著

中華民國三十六年

《冰期之庐山》英文版与中文版。

《冰期之庐山》一书是李四光将在庐山考察所得写成的专著。此书原稿完成于1937年，因受全民族抗日战争的影响，搁置十年，直至1947年才正式用中英文同时刊印发行。1937年李四光将此书的原稿交给英国《自然》杂志保存，1938年3月《自然》杂志以《中国中部的第四纪冰川》为题，撰文介绍李四光在庐山的冰川发现。

No. 3568, MARCH 19, 1938 NATURE 499

Quaternary Glaciations in Central China

DR. J. S. LEE, the well-known Chinese geologist, has sent to the Editor of NATURE the proofs of a monograph entitled "Quaternary Glaciations in the Lushan Area, Central China" with a series of photographs, intended in the first place for publication in vol. 2, ser. B, of *Academia Sinica*. Its transfer to England by air transport, with the request that it be placed in the safe custody of a responsible geological institution, conjures up a lively sense of the present and future state of affairs in China; which aspect, however, has no part in this article except in its bearing on the future publication of the monograph. Another aspect, and one having some significance, is that one would scarcely expect Dr. Lee to take such care to ensure the preservation of this material and to have it brought to the critical notice of expert glacialists, if he were not confident of the prime importance of his latest investigations in the Lushan mountain massif.

A few words of explanation are perhaps necessary to a proper understanding of the latter remarks. The very existence of evidences of glaciation in Central China has in the past been questioned by many geologists with experience of glaciated districts. When Dr. Lee in 1934 published his first account of the 'Boulder Clays', striated rocks, transported blocks, etc., in the Lower Yangtze Valley, and invoked true glaciation (as against solifluxion and allied phenomena) to explain the facts, his evidence was challenged by G. L. Barbour after a cursory joint traverse of the ground.

Barbour, while admitting the extraordinary character of many of the deposits, sought to identify them with long periods of abnormal subaerial weathering and erosion, possibly commencing as far back as early Pliocene or even Miocene times. The clay matrix of the 'Boulder Clay' was likened to non-glacial loam; the presence of boulders be explained as due to sinking into the leached soil of laterized surface rocks followed by gradual descent to lower ground under gravity; while a theoretical series of structural events was postulated to account for the presence of transported blocks in elevated positions relative to their apparent source. Further, an absence of (1) glacial sculpture, (2) glacio-fluviatile deposits, and (3) *roches moutonnées* was claimed by Barbour, though it was admitted that shortage of time prevented his seeing many crucial features.

At that time (1934), Barbour was clearly inclined to the belief that the glacial explanation of the Lushan phenomena was not acceptable. Yet he paid high compliment to Lee for "his penetrating recognition of the possible significance of this extraordinary geological occurrence", admitting further that the last word on the matter had not yet been said and that his (Lee's) interpretation had not been disproved.

That Dr. Lee was not deterred by these criticisms from a geologist of wide experience is shown by his energetic pursuit of confirmatory evidence, and the monograph under consideration directs attention to this glacial evidence under the headings (*a*) geomorphological indications; (*b*) moraines and their associated deposits; (*c*) striated rocks. A short account of the bed-rocks of the Lushan is given to enforce the arguments dealing with transported blocks; and more ambitious inferences than previously attempted are introduced to demonstrate a three-fold glaciation of the Yangtze valley.

A well-contoured map of the Lushan, bounded on the north by the Yangtze River and on the east by the Poyang Lake, accompanies the monograph. It shows the geographical extent of the glaciations and includes the observed indications of fluvio-glacial deposits, terminal and lateral moraines, drainage channels, glacial striæ, and striated boulders. The scale of the map is 1 : 50,000.

A critical review of the monograph is thought to be undesirable here. For it is clear that, failing an intimate knowledge of the area, an unquestioning acceptance of the validity of the glacial terminology must precede any attempt to estimate the full value of the evidence. This assumption is supported by the fact that G. L. Barbour, well experienced in low-latitude glacial phenomena, was unable to put forward final and convincing conclusions regarding the Lushan deposits and allied features. Attention will therefore be confined to a summary of the chief points of interest raised by Dr. Lee. Glacial geologists, by permission of the Editor of NATURE in arrangement with the Director of the Geological Survey and Museum, will be afforded the opportunity of consulting the monograph and map at the Survey Library, where the documents are being housed pending further instructions from Dr. Lee.

In his analysis of the glacial evidence, Dr. Lee stresses the fact that landforms have suffered extensive erosion and consequent modification since the last glacial period. The geomorphological indications are therefore not in themselves conclusive; but they were sufficient to inspire Lee and induce him to search for other signs of glacial

No. 3568, MARCH 19, 1938 NATURE 501

case of two "zungenbecken" or "central basins" relics of piedmont glaciers on the north side of the mountain.

Coming now to the important matter of depositional evidence, that is, moraines, boulder-clay, etc., we are presented with an interesting story leading to the postulation of three glaciations, associated with three distinct types of boulder-clay. The two lowland types are illustrated in Fig. 1, which shows the incorporation of blocks of the earlier well consolidated dark red variety by the later brick-red less consolidated one. The latter is more widespread and has undergone less laterization. It is important to note, in view of Barbour's earlier objection that the boulders in the boulder-clay were invariably hard quartzites and grit, that Lee now emphasizes their lithological variety. Lateral and terminal moraines, a block moraine, and an outwash apron are instanced, though a fuller development of these is said to be lacking as a result of excessive, inter- and post-glacial destruction. Solifluxion has been found inadequate to explain the transfer of large blocks over the long distances required; the famous Poyang Lake section of glacial drift containing such boulders is 9 km. from their source in the Lushan, and the intervening pre-glacial gradient is negligible, yet is, according to Lee, demonstrably greater than in Boulder Clay times.

Finally, the scratched boulders and striated rock surfaces (Fig. 2) are claimed by Lee to be perhaps the most convincing evidence for glacial operation, and it need only be remarked that Barbour's scepticism on this matter must have created in Lee a strong urge to test this type of evidence very thoroughly.

W. L.

Obituary Notices

Dr. G. E. Hale, For.Mem.R.S.

英国《自然》杂志上刊登的文章“*Quaternary Glaciations in Central China*”（《中国中部的第四纪冰川》）。

冰碛层。

鄱阳湖白石嘴冰川划痕。

李四光在桂林期间，几乎每年都要到重庆去参加一次中央研究院院务会议。蒋介石为了拉拢知识界，在会议结束时，总要宴请与会人员。李四光每次都借口有病或连夜离开，拒绝参加。有一次，李四光的座位被安排在蒋介石的旁边。蒋介石问翁文灏：“李四光先生怎么没有来？”翁文灏回答说：“重感冒，发烧。”过了一会儿，蒋介石又问陶孟和。陶孟和也说：“李先生病了。”这是1951年3月翁文灏从法国回到祖国后亲自对李四光讲的。1971年1月，翁文灏逝世，李四光还一直记得这件事，并十分感激地说：“翁文灏曾救过我一条命。”

1938年秋，桂林科学实验馆在良丰成立，李四光担任馆长。该馆由广西省政府与中央研究院合办，作为“研究解决广西省建设上实际问题之实验及设计机关”。科学实验馆与广西大学遥遥相对。1940年8月，广西大学校长马君武去世。李四光闻讯，深感悲痛。“将近四十年来的旧事，和着眼泪在脑海中翻来覆去，既不能忘，不如藉此机会付诸笔墨。”于是写下了《追念君武先生几件小故事》的悼念文章。在李四光饱经风霜的经历中，这类回忆往事的文章，是极为少见的。

经过几年的努力，科学实验馆虽然受到战时种种条件的限制，但还是初具规模地建立起来。1941年7月，李四光在广西《建设研究》杂志上发表了

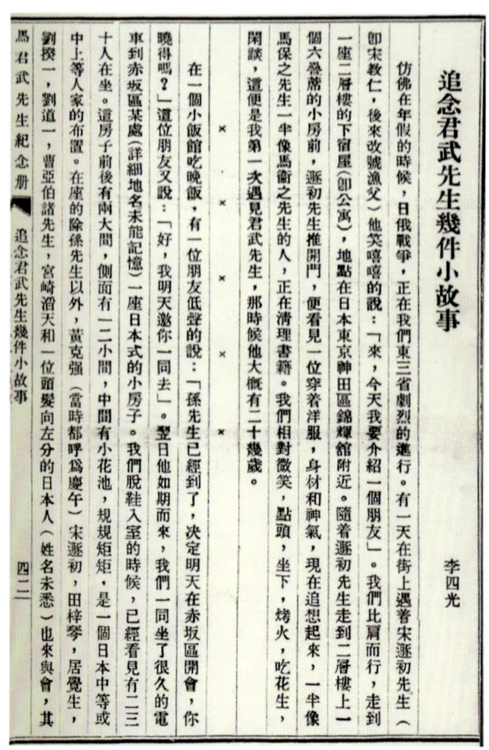

追念君武先生幾件小故事

李四光

彷彿在年假的時候，日俄戰爭，正在我們東三省劇烈的進行。有一天在街上遇着宋遯初先生（即宋教仁，後來改號漁父）他笑嘻嘻的說：「來，今天我要介紹一個朋友」。我們比肩而行，走到一座二層樓的下宿屋（即公寓），地點在日本東京神田區錦輝館附近。隨着遯初先生走到二層樓上一個六疊蓆的小房前，遯初先生推開門，便看見一位穿着洋服，身材和神氣，現在追想起來，一半像馬保之先生一半像馬衛之先生的人，正在清理書籍。我們相對微笑，點頭，坐下，烤火，吃花生，閑談，這便是我第一次遇見君武先生，那時候他大概有二十幾歲。

× × × × ×

在一個小飯館吃晚飯，有一位朋友低聲的說：「孫先生已經到了，決定明天在赤坂區開會，你曉得嗎？」這位朋友又說：「好，我明天邀你一同去」。翌日他如期而來，我們一同坐了很久的電車到赤坂區某處（詳細地名未能記憶）一座日本式的小房子。我們脫鞋入室的時候，已經看見有二三十人在坐。這房子前後有兩大間，側面有一二小間，中間有小花池，規規矩矩，是一個日本中等或中上等人家的布置。在座的除孫先生以外，黃克强（當時都呼爲慶午）宋遯初，田梓琴，居覺生，劉揆一，劉道一，曹亞伯諸先生，宮崎滔天和一位頭髮向左分的日本人（姓名未悉）也來與會，其

馬君武先生紀念册　追念君武先生幾件小故事　四二

《马君武先生纪念册》封面与书影。

马君武是李四光经宋教仁介绍在日本认识，同时加入同盟会的老朋友。1937年，全民族抗日战争全面爆发，李四光和地质研究所从庐山搬到桂林，和时任广西大学校长的马君武先生共同创办了“广西科学实验馆”。1940年马君武先生去世，李四光撰文回忆他和马君武先生相识、相交的经历。

《桂林科学实验馆概况》一文。同期发表的，还有欧阳予倩介绍广西省立艺术馆概况的文章。该刊在编后语中指出："桂林科学实验馆与省立艺术馆，可说是本省文化建设上的两个创举。"

1939年6月，《武汉日报》刊登湖北省政府关于临时参议会第一届参议员名单的通告。石瑛被任命为议长，李四光被任命为副议长。李四光对于这种参议会，并不感兴趣。9月，在当时湖北省政府所在地恩施举行的参议会第一次大会，李四光即电函请假。电文说："因事及交通困难，不克出席。"1940年4月，又要举行第二次大会，通知说石瑛议长有病，请李四光副议长主持。这时，李四光正在重庆，刚开完中国地质学会第16次年会。不得已，只好从重庆坐船到巴东。湖北省政府派来一辆烧木炭的汽车，把李四光接到恩施。李四光只代石瑛主持了参议会的一半议程，没有发表什么讲话。大会一结束，李四光就带着助手，从恩施出发，到湘西丘陵地域考察。一路上，参加参议会的那种沉闷心情，早已消失无遗。考察结束后，李四光回到桂林，即发电报给湖北省政府，请辞临时参议会副议长之职。湖北省政府主席陈诚给李四光复电慰留。但是，李四光辞退副议长的决心已下。此后，参议会举行的第三次和第四次大会，李四光均不出席。直到1941年临时参议会改组，举行第二届第一次大会，才正式接受了李四光的辞职。

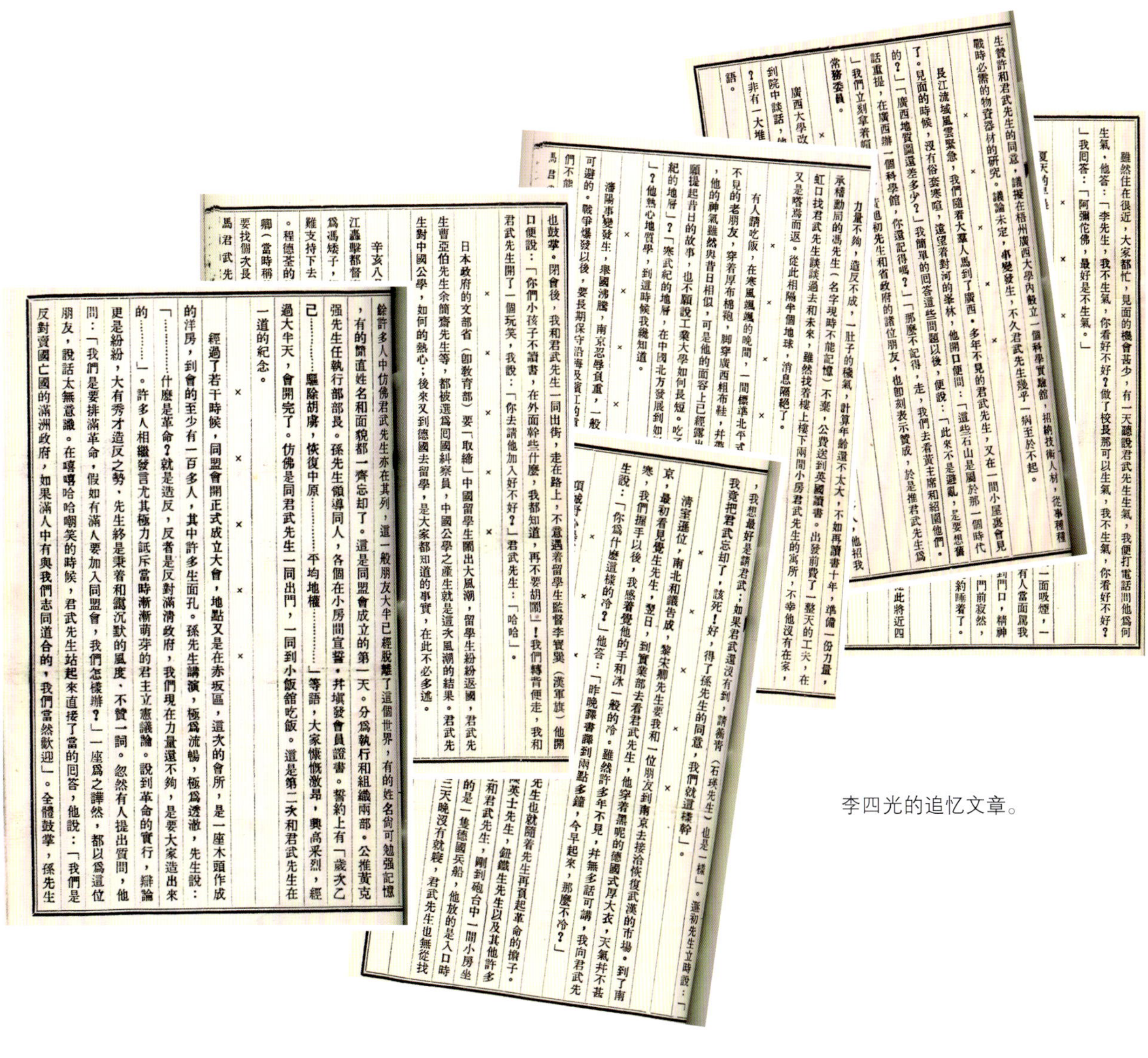

李四光的追忆文章。

1939年李四光（左一）、斯行健、俞建章、张文佑、
吴磊伯在黎塘镇龙山顶调查广西山字型构造。

在地质研究所迁到桂林的时候，李四光曾同大家商议，决定今后工作以鄂西、湘西、广西为范围。因为这一地域，矿产极为丰富，而详细情形迄今尚不甚明了。根据这样一个方针，地质研究所在这段时间里，工作的内容除研究地层和地质构造外，特别注重矿产资源的寻找和开发，其中对煤、铜、铁等矿种尤为注意。

南岭是长江流域和珠江流域之间断断续续山脉的统称。作为这样重要的天然界线或分水岭，在地理上南岭的存在是毫无问题的，然而在地质构造上的南岭究竟是否存在？如果存在，南岭究竟在何处？仿佛没有着落。为了弄清这个问题，早在1932年，李四光曾带着助手，从南京出发，分为四队深入湘桂境内，横断南岭中部进行过一次考察，所得的第一手资料十分丰富，可以说是了解南岭的起点。在桂林期间，李四光又对南岭做过两次考察。一次是1941年秋，他深入赣南、闽西、粤北地区，考察南岭东段，历时两个月。另一次是1942年春，由桂林经衡阳、郴州到资兴等地，考察南岭西段。经过这两次考察，李四光认为“就迄今得到的事实而言，南岭各部分的详细构造，虽然仍不甚明了，然而大致的看起来，可算已经有点头绪”。他发现这个地区的东西向构造、山字型构造、新华夏系构造等，有相互纷扰的现象。根据这些现象，李四光总结出“构造体系复合”的概念。1943年3月，中国地质学会在重庆举行第19次年会，李四光寄去了《南岭东段之主要构造型式及其各部分相互干涉之现象》一文，请人在会上代为宣读。

1942年7月，李四光的学生、在中央大学任教的朱森（字子元）在重庆不幸逝世，终年仅41岁。他是因其夫人误领五斗平价米，被人告奸而受到教育部所谓“贪污”的处分，气愤之下，胃溃疡恶化，以致不治而亡的。朱森的死，当时轰动了重庆，激起了知识界的愤慨和同情。《新华日报》专门为此发表了题为《论朱森教授之死》的社论。在桂林，李四光闻讯，百感交集。他毅然接见新闻记者，发表了义正词严的谈话。指出：“做地质工作的人们，本来就准备接受饿死、热死、跌死、打死、咬死、累死，尤其是这个时期，有什么说头？不过要说是气死，则国家无谓的牺牲未免太大。死了还要受气，更是太不成话！”

为了纪念朱森，8月，李四光发表了《朱森蜓·蜓科之一新属》的论文。指出：“这个新属名，是为了纪念已故的朱森教授而命名的，特别是为了纪念他在中国地层学上重要的贡献。”12月，李四光又发表《南岭何在》一文，追忆1932年他和朱森等结伴考察南岭山脉的艰难经历。文章的开头是一首五言诗《悼子元》：“崎岖五岭路，嗟君从我游。峰壑隐复见，环绕湘水头。风云忽变色，瘴疠蒙金瓯。山兮复何在，石迹耿千秋。”这深沉悲壮的诗句，表达了李四光对朱森的绵绵哀思，也表达了他对反动势力的重重怨恨。

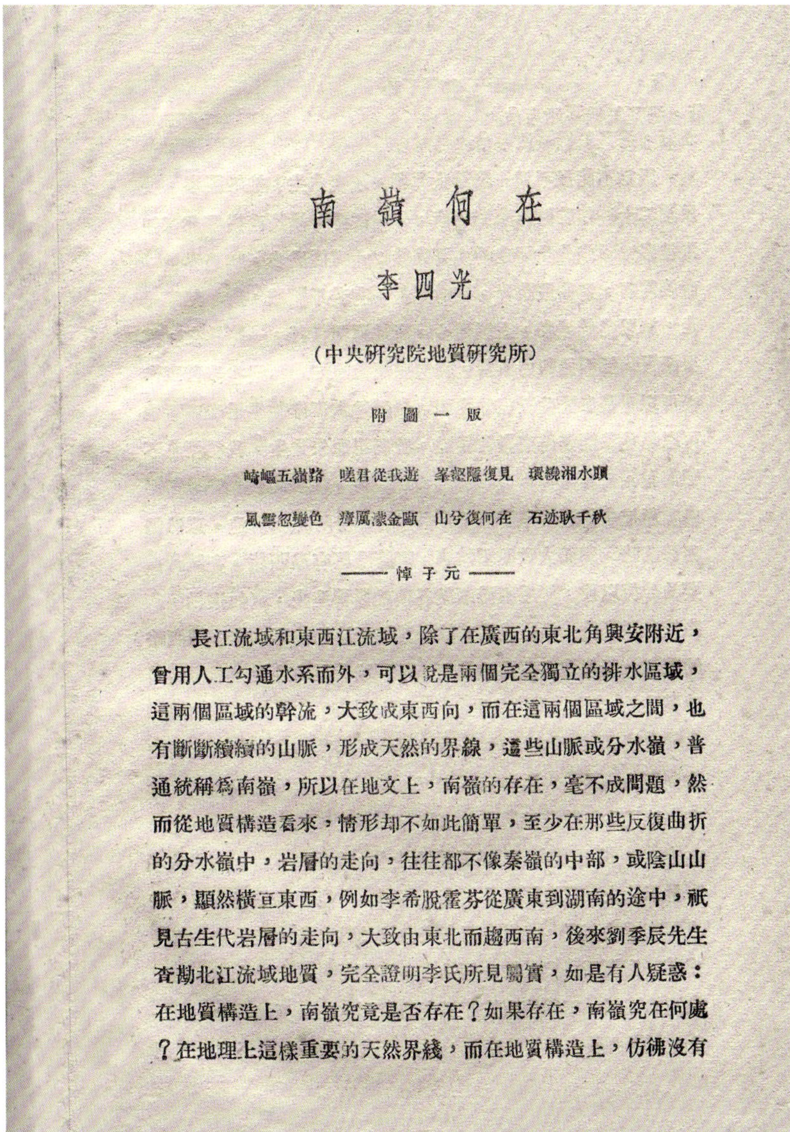

南嶺何在

李四光

（中央研究院地質研究所）

附圖一版

崎嶇五嶺路　嗟君從我遊　峯壑隱復見　環繞湘水頭

風雲忽變色　瘴厲濛金甌　山兮復何在　石迹耿千秋

——悼子元——

長江流域和東西江流域，除了在廣西的東北角興安附近，曾用人工勾通水系而外，可以說是兩個完全獨立的排水區域，這兩個區域的幹流，大致成東西向，而在這兩個區域之間，也有斷斷續續的山脈，形成天然的界線，這些山脈或分水嶺，普通統稱為南嶺，所以在地文上，南嶺的存在，毫不成問題，然而從地質構造看來，情形却不如此簡單，至少在那些反復曲折的分水嶺中，岩層的走向，往往都不像秦嶺的中部，或陰山山脈，顯然横亘東西，例如李希脫霍芬從廣東到湖南的途中，祇見古生代岩層的走向，大致由東北而趨西南，後來劉季辰先生查勘北江流域地質，完全證明李氏所見屬實，如是有人疑惑：在地質構造上，南嶺究竟是否存在？如果存在，南嶺究在何處？在地理上這樣重要的天然界綫，而在地質構造上，仿彿沒有

1942年12月李四光发表《南岭何在》一文，文章开头是一首五言诗《悼子元》。

1945年李四光夫妇在重庆。

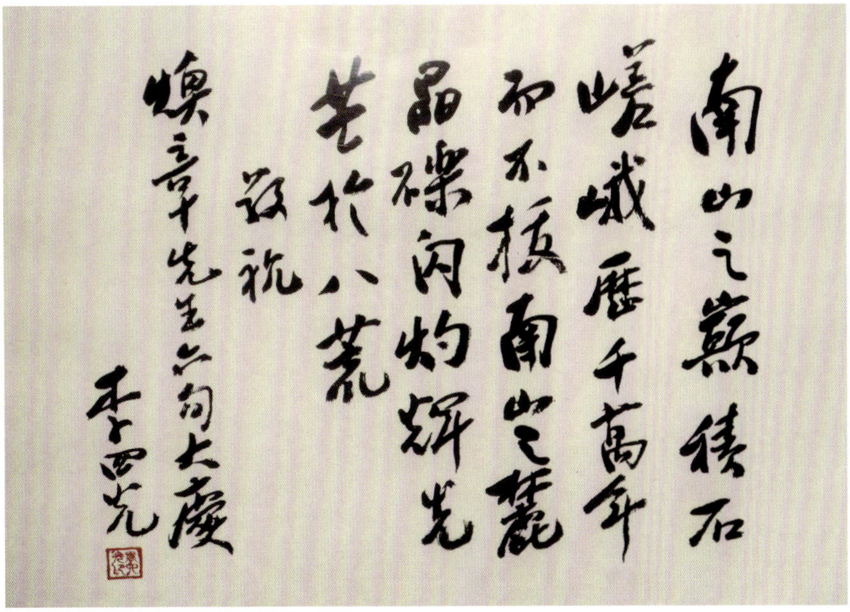

1942年李四光写给冯玉祥的祝寿信。

进入1944年，日本侵略军在太平洋战场上节节失利。为了挽救其失败的命运，自4月起从河南开始发动大规模的军事行动，力图由北向南打通大陆交通线。而这时的国民党军队却实行大撤退。在短时间里，大片国土沦丧，数千万同胞流离失所。

到了6月，日军从湘桂路直扑桂林。这里不能久留了。李四光考虑，在这外侵内患的动乱年月，恐怕只能走一步看一步了。他即率地质研究所同事，携带轻便的物品，仓促离开桂林，开始了奔波的苦难旅程。李四光在途中不幸染上了痢疾，身体十分虚弱。火车到了独山，在夫人许淑彬的一位远亲帮助下，搞到了一辆卡车。一路上，走走停停。就这样，20多天后，才到贵阳。在乐湾万松阁附近的一座古庙里，设立了地质研究所办事处。到了10月，独山失守，都匀吃紧，眼看贵阳就要被围困。李四光和他的同事，只好再行奔波。他们从贵阳出发，经过遵义，11月抵达重庆。借用四川地质调查所的房屋，把地质研究所安置下来。李四光夫妇暂时居住在沙坪坝租到的一栋小楼房里。

1945年1月11日，是蔡元培诞辰纪念日（他于1940年3月5日在香港病逝，此后每逢其诞辰，文化教育界总要为他举行隆重的纪念）。这一天，中央研究院和重庆大学、北京大学同学会联合举行蔡元培诞辰纪念会，到会共有300多人。李四光应邀在会上做了《从地质力学观点上看中国山脉之形成》的学术演讲。演讲时间原定下午。会议主持者中央研究院院长朱家骅在上午的会上，请李四光对下午的演讲内容做一个题解说明。李四光即席用生动而通俗的话，做了一个颇能引人入胜的题解。他说："世界上大小山脉很多，何以能够形成这些大大小小的山脉？这是一个国家内的问题，也是一个世界的问题。""要解决中国山脉问题非解决世界上的山脉问题不可。"他还说：这个问题初看上去是属于地质学范围，但是单单依靠地质学并不能解答，必须得到其他学科的配合研究才能去弄明白。他自己研究山脉的形成，就是运用地质力学方法来解决的。

1945年4—5月，重庆大学和中央大学联合举行学术报告会，约请李四光做学术演讲。李四光这次演讲前后共五次，系统地讲述了他20多年悉心研究的地质力学。这次演讲稿，经过整理后，李四光正式命题为《地质力学之基础与方法》，首先由重庆大学地质系印发。1947年1月才正式由中华书局作为中国科学社丛书之一出版发行。任何一门科学理论的创立，都是从实践中来的。李四光在创立地质力学这门新兴学科之前，进行了大量的地质实践，在地层学、古生物学、岩石学以及构造地质学等方面，做了广泛的调查和细致的研究，取得了出色的成就。仅地质构造运动的名称，由他命名的，不下十四五个之多。其中有些名称，一直袭用到今天。

由于长期的颠沛流离、过度的紧张工作，李四光的身体终于不支，心脏病发作了。这一年，他56岁。他来到北碚著名的北温泉疗养。第二年11月，由重庆乘船东下，到上海就医。1947年9月，又由上海到杭州养病。

这时，李四光一边养病，一边仍在工作。1945年8月，日本宣布投降后，他立即派人到南京，接收地质研究所原有的房屋和设备，并到庐山清查存放的物品。原来借调到外单位去的同事，现在又陆续回所了。这样，全所人员比1937年11月离开南京时还要多一些，一共有30多人了。1946年10月，中国地质学会在南京举行第22次年会，到会110人，李四光因病不能出席主持，也不能按照惯例亲自在会上发表理事长的学术演讲。他只好口述题为《中韩沿海与大陆破裂》的论文节要，请他的学生、地质研究所代理所长兼重庆大学地质系主任俞建章记录，赶寄年会。参加年会的会员听到后都很感动，立即发电，向李四光表示慰问。

1946年4月5日李四光夫妇（右一、右二）在渝北温泉与学生胡伦积等合影。

回到新中国

Returning Home

(1947—1950)

1947年冬李四光夫妇与友人在上海。

1947年6—7月，中国地质学会理事会在南京举行会议，讨论参加1948年在伦敦举行的第18届国际地质大会参会代表的问题。会议决定，用通信方法，由全体理事票选两人。结果，李四光、尹赞勋当选。后来，国民党政府教育部以经费短缺为理由，只批准了李四光一人参加。

1948年在香港和老朋友陈厚甫一家。

1948年在香港老朋友陈厚甫家门前合影。

1948年2月，李四光从上海启程赴伦敦，准备参加第18届国际地质大会，夫人许淑彬一同前往。他们从上海到香港候船，直到4月初，才搭上一艘挪威货轮。海行两月有余，抵达法国南岸马赛。在马赛上岸，坐火车经巴黎去伦敦。当时在剑桥大学攻读博士学位的女儿李林，已早早来到多佛尔码头等候，并在伯明翰附近租好了一间房子，把父母安顿下来。

1948年在香港老朋友陈厚甫家。

1948年在香港和老朋友陈厚甫的女儿（中）合影。

第18届国际地质大会理事合影。第二排右起第13人是李四光，第12人是李夫人许淑彬。

国际地质大会当时已有70多年的历史。1933年在华盛顿举行的第16届国际地质大会上，李四光发表了《东亚构造格架》一文；1937年在莫斯科举行的第17届国际地质大会上，李四光发表了《中国震旦纪冰川》一文；这一届国际地质大会上，李四光将亲自宣读论文《新华夏海的起源》。李四光所称的新华夏海，是指东亚东缘的渤海、黄海、东海和日本海。他认为，研究新华夏海的起源，对于弄清太平洋盆地的发育，有重要的意义。

李四光夫妇在伦敦参加第18届国际地质大会期间。

1 | 2 / 3

1、2、3—李四光夫妇在伦敦参加第18届国际地质大会期间。

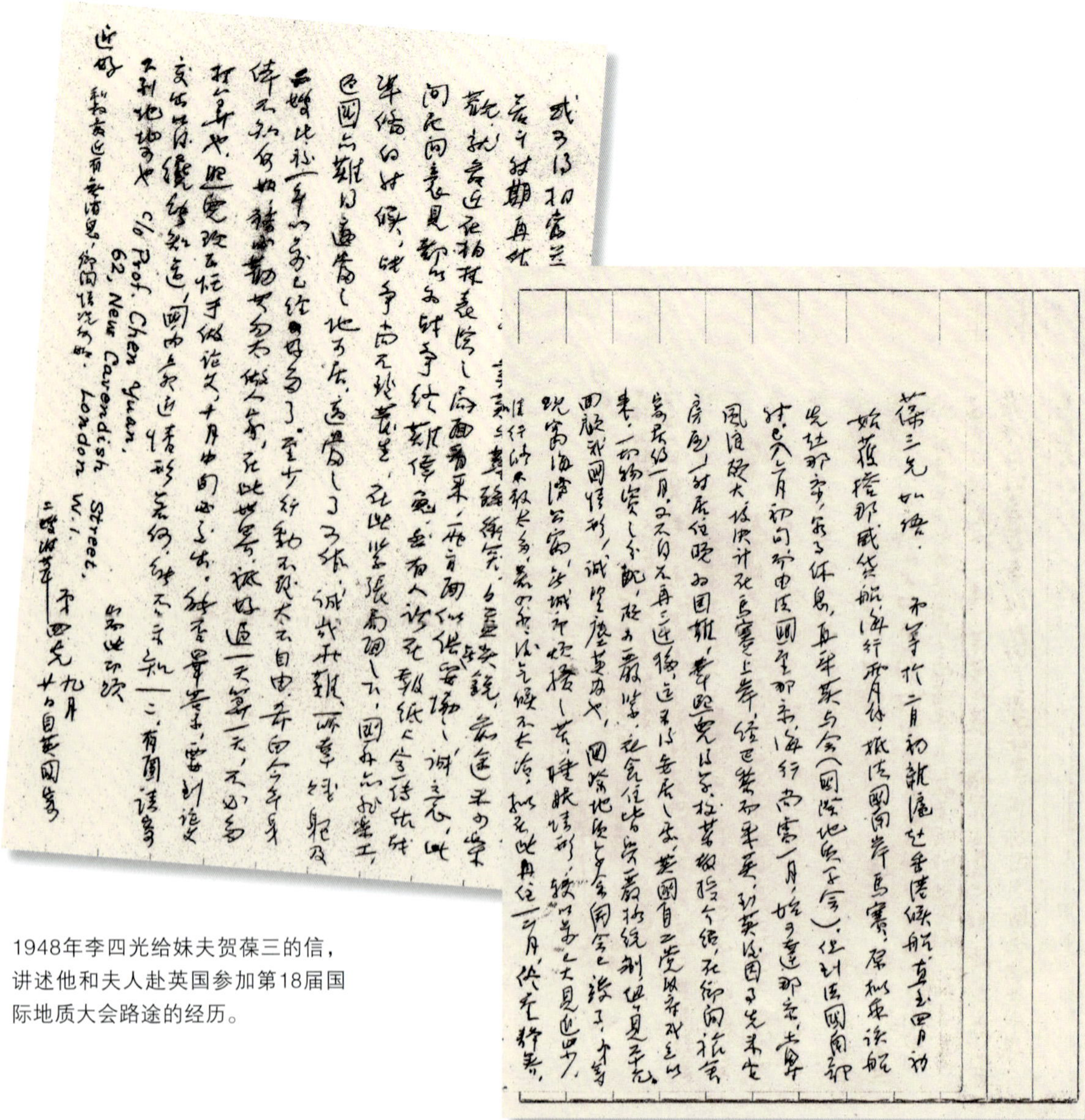

1948年李四光给妹夫贺葆三的信，讲述他和夫人赴英国参加第18届国际地质大会路途的经历。

国际地质大会结束之后，李四光没有立即回国。他同夫人迁到了伯恩茅斯海湾公寓，继续静养身体，同时观察国内外时局的发展。1948年9月20日，李四光在给妹夫贺有年（贺葆三）的信中说：就最近柏林问题看来，“美英与苏联冲突日益尖锐，前途未可乐观”。“在此紧张局面之下，国内亦非乐土，返国亦难得适当之地可居，适当之工作可做，诚哉两难。”因此，他打算，如果英伦的气候太冷，“则拟赴法国或瑞士休息若干时期，再作计划”。

然而祖国的解放战争进展速度之快，远远超出了李四光的预料。1949年元旦过后，国民党政府仓皇逃往广州，并命令各机关南迁。地质研究所被通知搬迁到广州中山大学。一时人心惶惶，不知所从。1月13日，地质研究所许杰、赵金科秘密协商起草了一个反对搬迁的誓约。在这个誓约上签字的有11人。他们将这个情况，写信告诉了李四光。

李四光从1月19日至2月9日，分别给许杰、赵金科和俞建章等写过三封信，发过一个电报。他对许杰、赵金科等“愿留守本所，看护书籍、仪器，深为钦佩”。至于搬到广州中山大学的问题，李四光说：如果因为要同中山大学合作，“只好任有志者前往”；若为地质研究所及同人避乱，“似无多意义，我个人绝不赞成”。信中还说到，现在是青黄不接的时候，最可虑者，是同人的柴米等各项生活问题。并表示愿将个人名下所存的少许积资公开，“作本所作研究工作同人救济之用，箪食瓢饮，或尚可维持于一时，俟局面稍定，再从长计议可也”。由于李四光的力阻和地质研究所留守南京同人的努力，这场反搬迁斗争胜利了。4月23日，南京解放时，地质研究所没有受到一点损失，完整地回到了人民的怀抱。

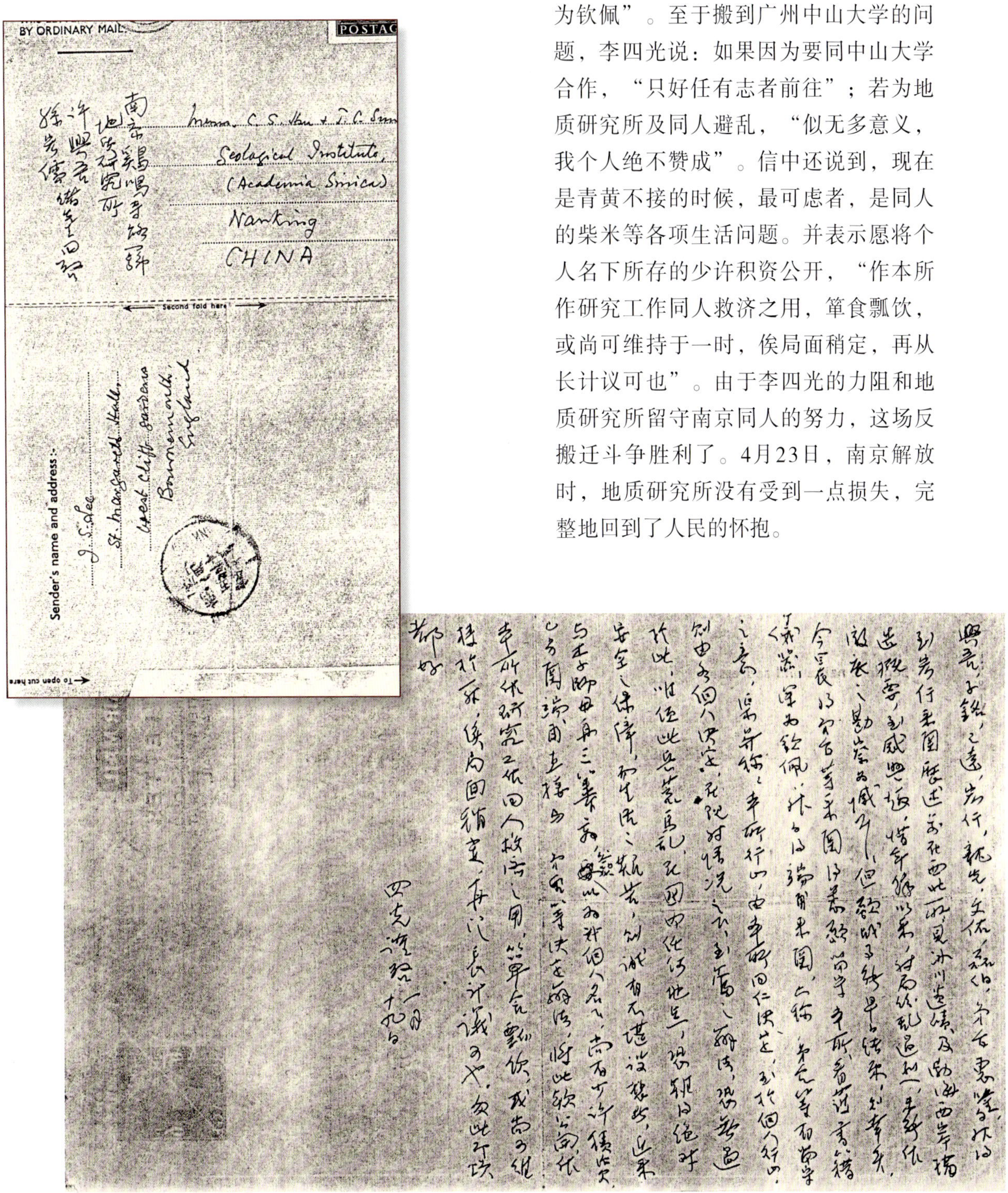

1949年1月李四光给地质研究所同人的信，表明他绝不赞成搬迁的态度，并提出将他个人所存的积资公开，作为研究所的工作和个人救济之用。

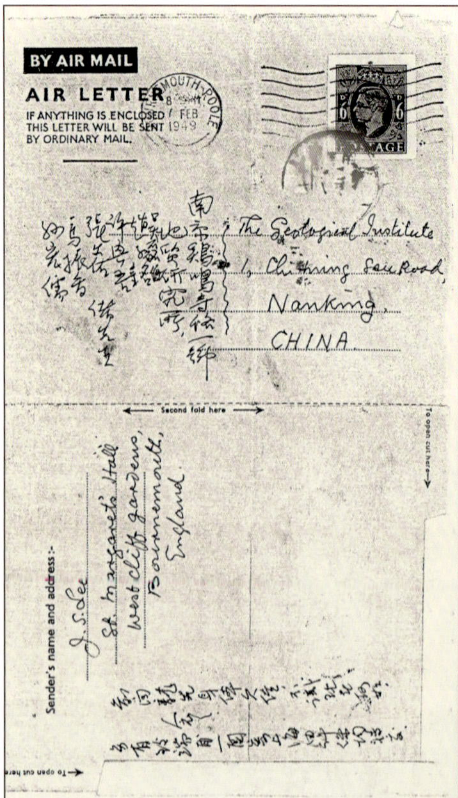

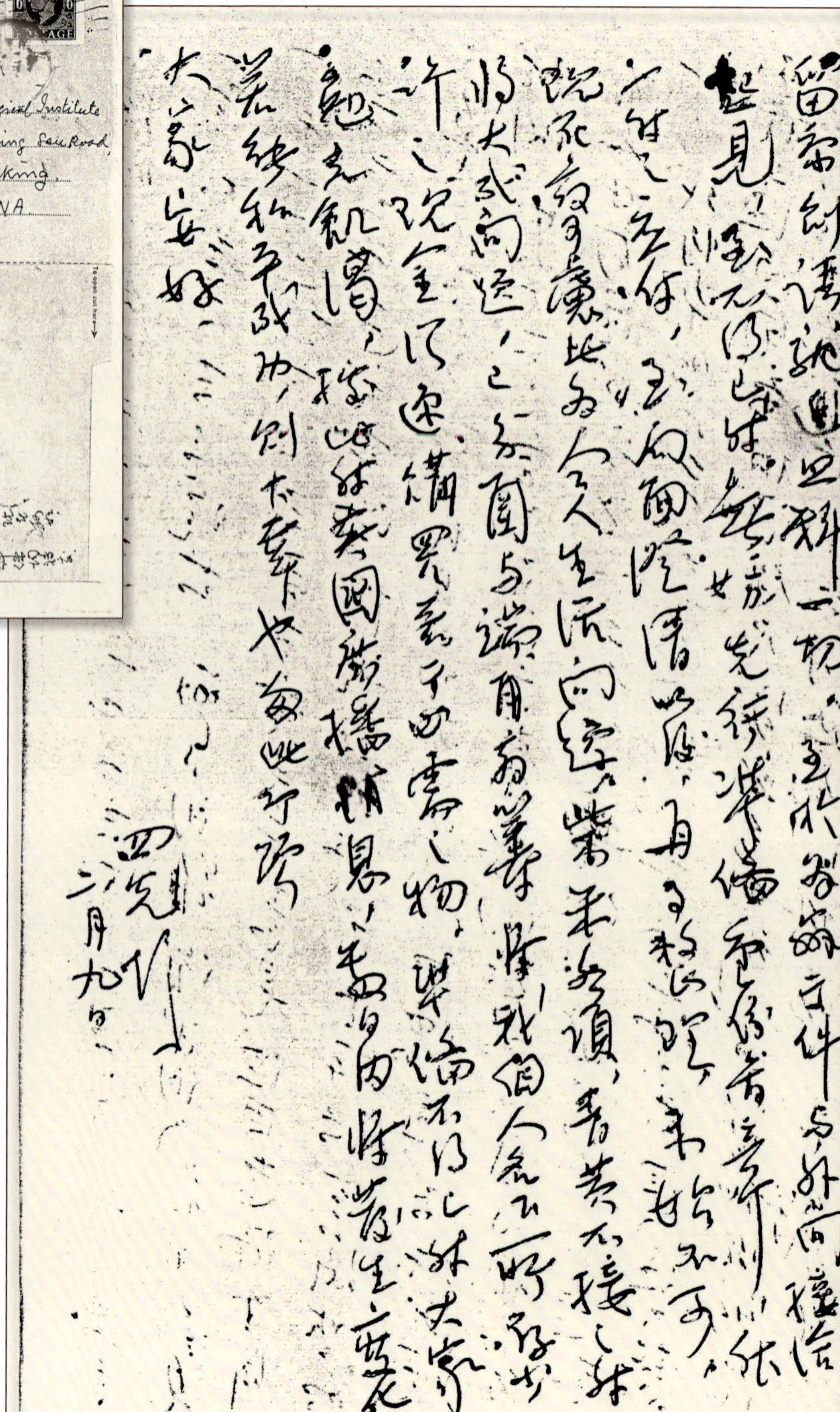

1949年2月李四光再次写信给地质研究所同人，希望大家留在原地，不要搬迁。

子铭、贤君、乐佑、岩仟、之远、及其他留英同仁共鉴：　顷得编甫

一函，颇虑及本院脱节，两予困难，俾我们个人表示意见，

因于此次迁移问题，前曾有发表弟之意见，但因远隔重洋，

恐所云所论未必适合实际情况，故暂不予置论，所务会议结果的

人决定：既在今后一时期地点仍为上海，即稳定，弟将我个人

想到：中山大学之合作，在纯方面要同该所取消，我方抵押任

有害于前途，且应讲求合作之基础，若为两所各人之遗利，

计：我将本所求合作中迁至广州，则似无多意义，但个人绝不赞成，

至于上海与南京，相隔不过咫尺，能多帮助，为与其他诸所取得

联系，拟请编甫代筹急需物件，以上一切，

1949年暑假李四光参加留英中国学生会年会。第二排左十是李四光，第三排右六是李四光的女婿邹承鲁。

中央研究院为李四光六秩寿辰出了一本纪念增刊，许多人写了纪念文章，卷首是中国地质事业奠基人、年高德劭的章鸿钊写的一曲《南乡一剪梅》墨迹影印专页。

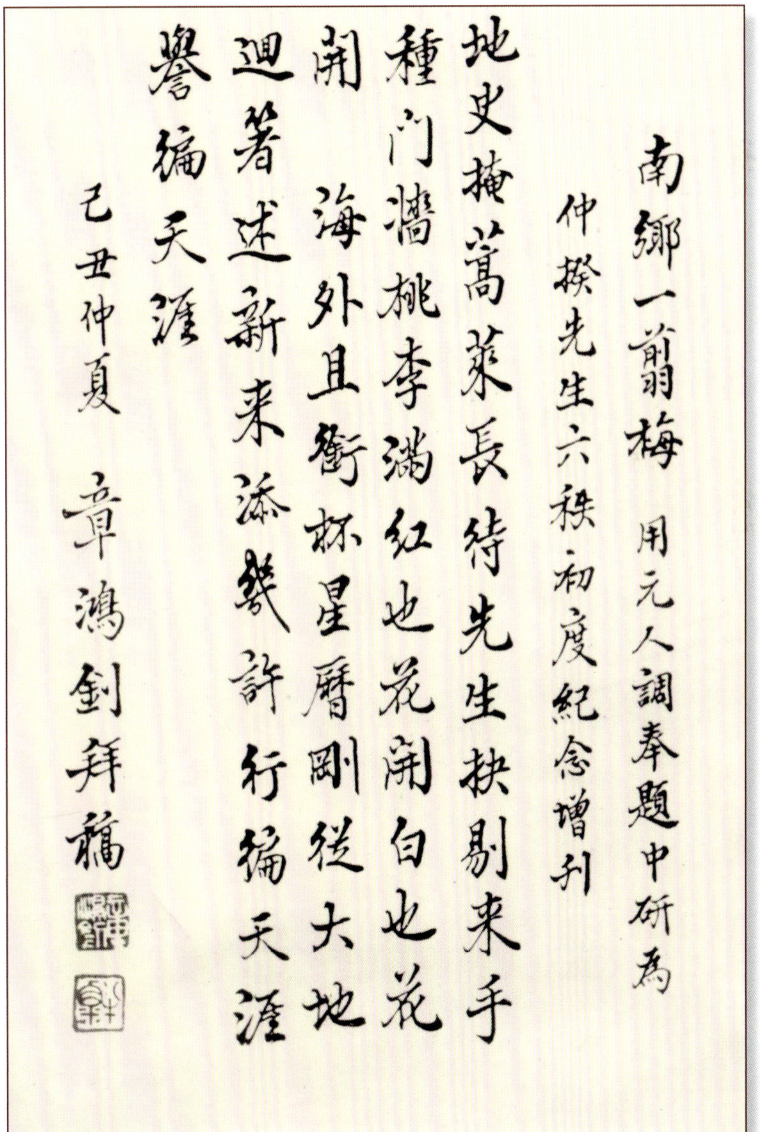

南鄉一翦梅　用元人調奉題中研為
仲揆先生六秩初度紀念增刊
地史掩蒿萊長待先生抉剔来手
種门牆桃李滿红也花開白也花
開　海外且銜杯星曆剛從大地
廻著述新来添幾許行徧天涯
譽徧天涯
己丑仲夏　章鴻釗拜稿

女儿结婚时一家四口的合影。这张照片的四个人中有三个日后成为中国科学院院士，被誉为“一门三院士”。

女儿李林结婚时的全家合影。

4月初，以郭沫若为团长的中国代表团赴布拉格出席世界维护和平大会。出国前，郭沫若根据周恩来的指示，给李四光带了一封信。这封信是郭沫若带头签署的，内容是请李四光早日返国。李四光在英国接到了这封信，心情自然十分激动。他马上订好了由马赛开往香港的船票，办好了过路的签证。但遗憾的是，那时由英国到远东的船很少，要等半年才能启程。这时，李四光夫妇想到了女儿的婚事，于是决定于8月26日，在伯恩茅斯，临时请了几位朋友，以简朴的仪式，为女儿李林和女婿邹承鲁举行了婚礼。邹承鲁当时也在剑桥大学攻读博士学位，他是学生物化学的；李林是学物理冶金的。他们学业结束后，都先后回到了祖国。

女儿结婚时父母的合影。

1949年李四光与妻子许淑彬、女儿李林在英国海滨城市伯恩茅斯。

1949年李四光和妻子、
女儿在伦敦海德公园。

1949年李四光与女儿
李林在伦敦。

李四光、许淑彬、李林和友人凌淑华（左五）等在伦敦的海德公园。

李四光一家在伦敦海德公园。

女儿订婚时在剑桥合影。左起：许淑彬、李林、李四光、邹承鲁。

在伯恩茅斯寓所前与参加女儿婚礼的陈源（陈西莹）一家合影。左起：李四光、陈小莹、陈源、凌淑华、许淑彬、李林和邹承鲁。

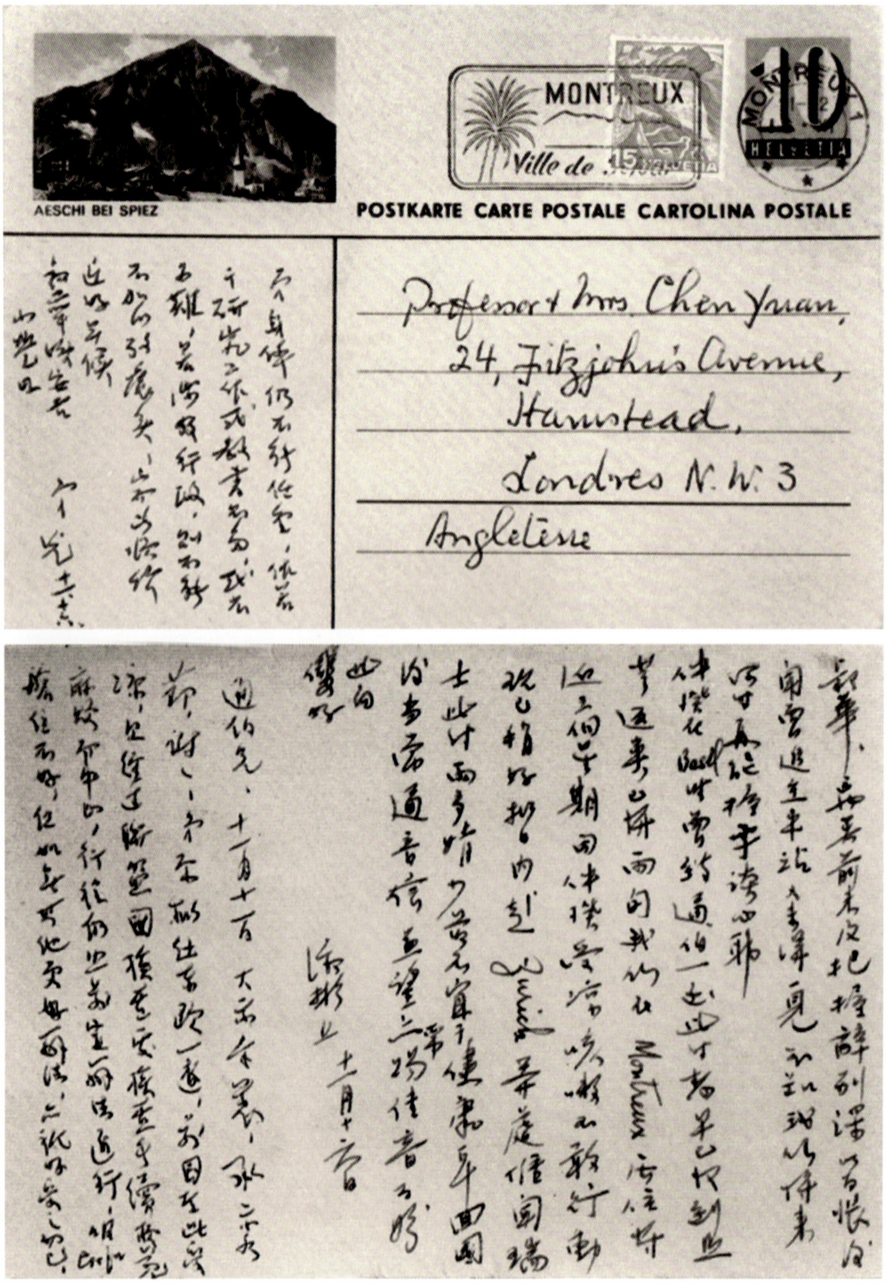

1949年11月归国途中李四光夫妇在瑞士写给老朋友陈源的信。

1949年9月，中国人民政治协商会议第一届全体会议在北平开幕。各地报纸在同日都公布了政协第一届全体会议的代表名单，分为党派代表、区域代表、军队代表、团体代表和特邀人士等，共662名。李四光是作为中华全国第一次自然科学工作者代表大会筹备委员会这个团体的代表之一，列入这届政协会议名单的。同时，李四光还被推选为中华全国第一次自然科学工作者代表大会筹备委员会常委会副主任委员。10月，中央人民政府委员会第三次会议通过，成立中国科学院，李四光被任命为副院长。

正当李四光以焦急的心情等待着启程的日期时，台湾国民党正在策划着一个阻挠李四光返回祖国的阴谋。一天，伦敦的一位朋友给李四光打来了一个电话，告诉他，“驻英大使”郑天锡接到国民党的密令，要李四光公开发表声明，拒绝接受中国共产党领导的全国政协委员的职务，不然就有被扣留的危险。

李四光在英国和老朋友陈源在一起。

事情发生的突然，促使李四光当机立断，他同夫人许淑彬商量了一下，就拿起一个小皮包，只身从普利茅斯渡过英伦海峡，到了法国。第二天，“国民党驻英大使馆”果然派人来找李四光，李夫人对来人说，李四光外出考察去了。过了两个星期，许淑彬收到李四光的来信，说他已到了瑞士与德国交界的巴塞尔。许淑彬明白，这是让她前去会合。

李四光夫妇在巴塞尔买好了从意大利的热那亚开往香港的船票，但离开船的日期，还有一个多月，他们趁此机会游历了罗马、庞贝古城及水上城市威尼斯等地。

1949年底归国途中李四光先行到达瑞士巴塞尔，许淑彬随后和他会合，一同回国。

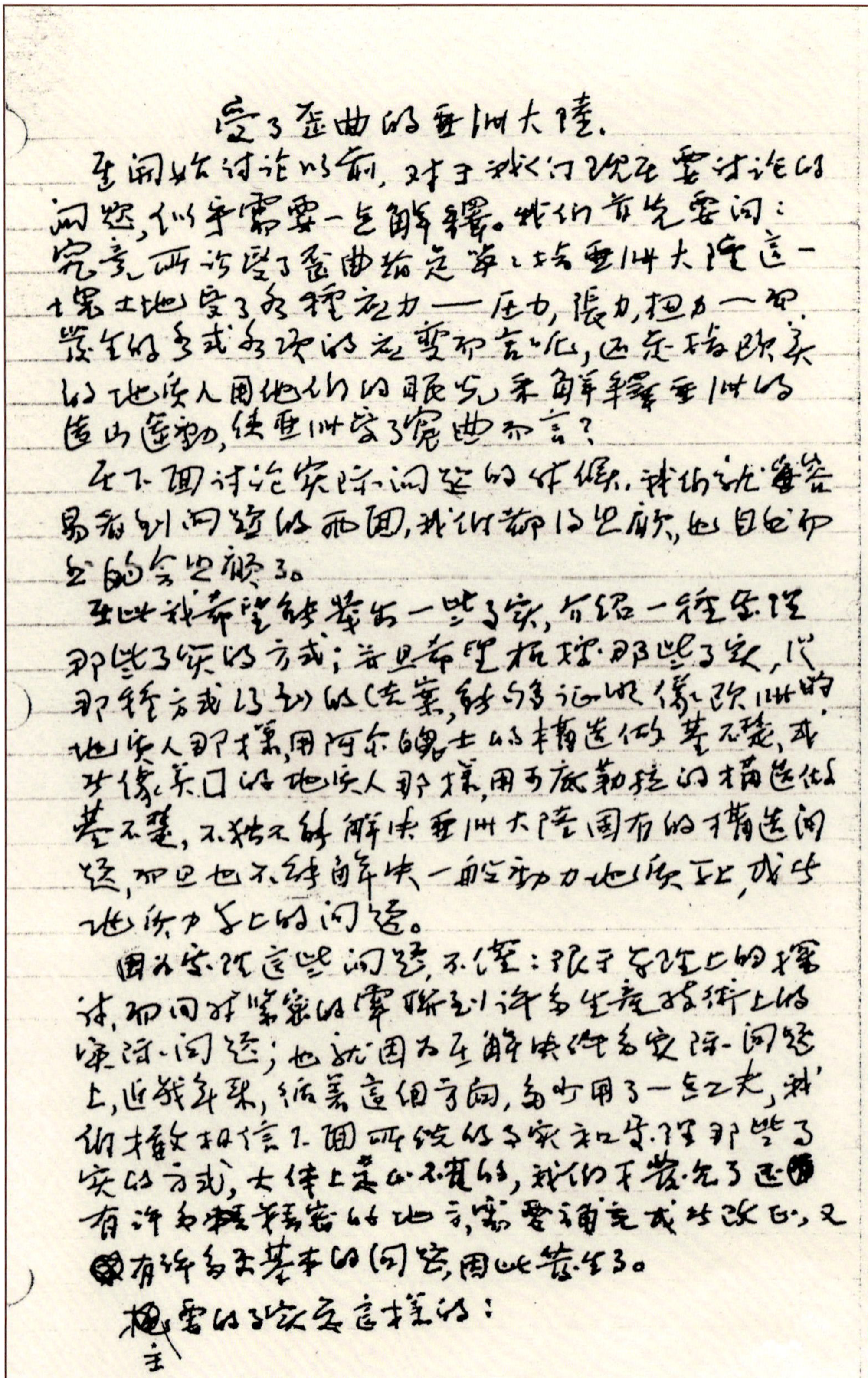

受了歪曲的亚洲大陆。

在开始讨论以前，对于我们现在要讨论的问题，似乎需要一点解释。我们首先要问：究竟所谓受了歪曲指的是亚洲大陆这一块土地受了各种应力——压力，张力，扭力——所发生的各式各样的变形而言呢，还是指欧美的地质人用他们的眼光来解释亚洲的造山运动，使亚洲受了歪曲而言？

在下面讨论实际问题的时候，我们就容易看到问题的两面，我们静以思考，也自然而然的会明显了。

在此我希望能举出一些事实，介绍一种说明那些事实的方式；并且希望根据那些事实，从那种方式得到的答案，能够证明像欧洲的地质人那样用阿尔卑斯的构造做基础，或者像美国的地质人那样用阿帕拉契的构造做基础，不独不能解决亚洲大陆固有的构造问题，而且也不能解决一般动力地质上，或者地质力学上的问题。

因为研究这些问题，不仅仅限于学理上的探讨，而同时紧密的牵联到许多生产技术上的实际问题；也就因为要解决许多实际问题，近几年来，沿着这个方向，多少用了一点工夫，我们确切相信下面所说的事实和说明那些事实的方式，大体上是正确的，我们不能免了还有许多粗糙的地方，需要补充或者改正，又有许多基本的问题，因此发生了。

概要的说来是这样的：

李四光著作《受了歪曲的亚洲大陆》中文稿手迹，
1951年此文在国内发表。

1949年12月25日，李四光和夫人许淑彬由热那亚启程秘密回国。在归国途中，为悼念已故的著名印度古植物学家萨尼（B. Sahni）教授，李四光写了《受了歪曲的亚洲大陆》一文。文章开头，用简洁而富于感情的词句，追述了他同萨尼的友谊，特别是在他处境困难的时刻，从萨尼那里得到的鼓舞。萨尼在古植物学方面的贡献是人所共知的，并且对其他科学领域也有广泛的兴趣。1945年秋天，当李四光在重庆病倒时，忽然接到萨尼的一封来信。那封信不仅表达了友谊的温暖，而且提出了一个富有启发性的课题，即期望得到导致印度东北急转弯那样奇异的地壳歪曲变形的连续进程的证据。这在不小的程度上，“给予一个为生活苦恼的人恢复了兴趣”。李四光很快地答应在一篇文章中，将对有关事实和推论做一次尝试性的总结，并在适当的时机，赠送给这位博学的印度同行。但是，将近五年过去了，曾经答应过的约定，“现在才有机会完成，虽然这是一个悲伤的任务”。

Intra-Tethyan Arcs versus Gondwanan Lineaments.

Aspects of Asiatic Arcs
Interpreted from Distortion of Clay.
by J. S. Lee

Students of Asiatic tectonics seem now generally agreed that the well known Suessian arcs are by no means all of the same type and the same origin. This may also be said of certain classes of Argand's virgations. There are however two distinct groups of arcs apparently originated from related movement of parts of the continent. They occur in chains, each being characterized by a specific type and oriented and distributed in a definite way.

Those which border on the continent with their convex front facing south-east may be conveniently described as peripacific, and those with their convex front facing south generally arrange themselves side by side traversing sinuously across the continent in an east-west direction and occasionally tandem from north to south. Because of this fact it appears not unsuitable to describe them as transcontinental. None of these has anything in common with that grandiose mountain arc sweeping round the western border of China past Burma, the Andaman and Nicobar Islands and finally incorpor-

《特提斯弧与冈瓦纳构造线对比——从黏土扭曲实验看亚洲的形态》英文讲演稿手迹。

1950年3月初，李四光和夫人许淑彬经过三个多月的重洋飘渡，终于到达了香港。到码头上接他们的是留日同学陈厚甫。当年李四光学造船，陈厚甫学土木，共同的志愿和邻近的学科，使他们朝夕相处，知己相许。后来，陈厚甫继承父业，在香港经商。这次陈厚甫在接到李四光从旅途中的来信之后，非常高兴，亲自到码头把李四光夫妇从船上接下来，随即把他们安置到预先准备好的一个僻静的住所。

李四光离开伦敦的消息，早已通过另外的途径传到了北京中南海。正在主持中央人民政府政务院工作的周恩来总理，更是关切李四光的旅途安全。1949年11月15日，周总理给新华通讯社驻布拉格分社社长吴文焘发去一封电报并告中国驻苏联大使王稼祥，电文说："李四光先生受反动政府压迫，已秘密离英赴东欧，准备返国，请你们设法与之接触。并先向捷克当局交涉，给李以入境便利，并予保护。"但是，11月27日，吴文焘给周总理回电说：李四光"尚无来捷消息"。

按行程计算，已经是该到达的时候了，为什么还没有消息呢？周总理把这个任务委托给以叶剑英为第一书记的中共中央华南分局。根据情况分析，李四光不可能走北路经苏联回来，因为他办不到签证；走南路，必经香港。从香港来往的朋友中，有可能了解到他的消息。那是一个上午，陈厚甫正在为李四光的安全回国向一位朋友打探消息的时候，对方也正好接受可靠朋友的委托，了解一位叫"Jes. Li"（李四光的英文名字叫"J. S. Lee"，介绍时，被听者听成了"Jes. Li"——编者注）的60岁上下的学者是否来到了香港。双方的高兴就不用说了，很快就做好了安排。就在陈厚甫和那位朋友约定后的第二天，李四光夫妇被送到一位陌生人的家里。主人告诉李四光："大陆上来了一位朋友麦可先生（即黎雪，曾任中国科学院科学出版社负责人——编者注），想和你谈谈。"李四光怎么也没有想到，这位从大陆来的人，是这么一位彬彬有礼而又能说一口流利英语的同胞。谈话持续了两个小时，分手前约定，两天后再见面。

1950年4月6日，李四光和夫人许淑彬一大早就起身，六点过后，他们已经坐在香港去九龙的轮渡上。到达九龙，李四光看到很快就要踏进解放了的新中国的南大门，心中有说不出的激动。

肩负重任

Laying the Foundations of Chinese Geology

(1950—1957)

李四光夫妇到达广州后的第二天，踏上了赴上海的旅途。由于连日的紧张劳累，李四光感到心脏不太舒服，在上海住了四天。1950年4月13日到达南京。李四光到达南京的消息在《新华日报》上登出后，由于他在国内国际科学界的声望，特别是他经过斗争，排除阻挠，终于回到祖国的爱国精神，使得许多文教科学单位的工作人员都很钦佩，都很希望能见到他，听他讲讲自己的迂回曲折的经历。李四光自己也因能回到祖国，与久别的科教界的同事们见面而感到高兴。但他究竟是已满60岁的人了，旅途的劳累尚未完全恢复，在组织的安排下，每隔一天才允许他参加半天的活动。

1950年4月13日李四光抵达南京，南京市委宣传部、军管会高教处负责人到车站迎接。

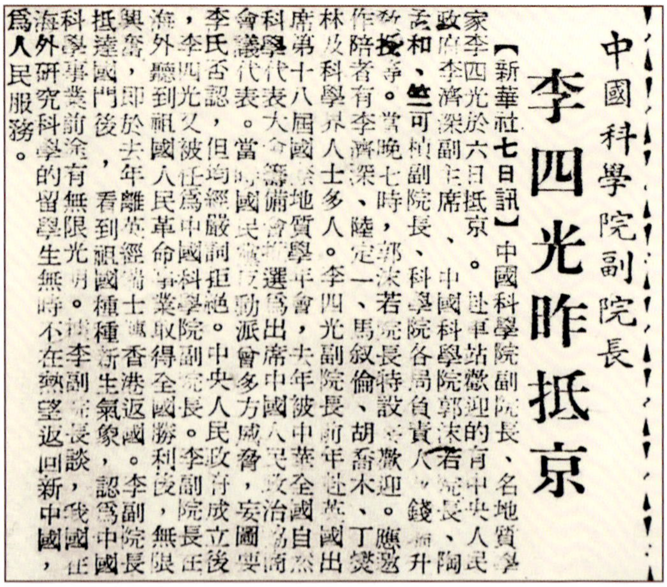

中國科學院副院長

李四光昨抵京

【新華社七日訊】中國科學院副院長、名地質學家李四光於六日抵京。赴車站歡迎的有中央人民政府李濟深副主席、中國科學院郭沫若院長、陶孟和、竺可楨副院長、科學院各局負責人，錢端升教授等。當晚七時，郭沫若院長特設宴歡迎。應邀作陪者有李濟深、陸定一、馬叙倫、胡喬木、丁燮林及科學界人士多人。李四光副院長前年赴英國出席第十八屆國際地質學年會，去年被中華全國自然科學代表大會籌備會選爲出席中國人民政治協商會議代表。當時國民黨反動派曾多方威脅，妄圖要李氏否認，但均經嚴詞拒絕。中央人民政府成立後，李四光又被任爲中國科學院副院長。李副院長在海外聽到祖國人民革命事業取得全國勝利後，無限興奮，即於去年離英經瑞士轉香港返國。李副院長抵達國門後，看到祖國種種新生氣象，認爲中國科學事業前途有無限光明。據李副院長談，我國在海外研究科學的留學生無時不在熱望返回新中國，爲人民服務。

1950年5月8日，《人民日报》发表消息，报道李四光回国。

5月6日，李四光和夫人到达北京。到火车站迎接的，有中央人民政府副主席、全国政协副主席、中国国民党革命委员会主席李济深，中央文教委员会主任委员、中国科学院院长郭沫若，副院长陶孟和、竺可桢，文化部副部长丁西林，北京大学教授钱端升，中财委计划局副局长钱昌照等。当晚，郭沫若设宴招待，李济深、陆定一、马叙伦、胡乔木、丁西林、华罗庚、谢家荣等作陪，新老相识欢聚一堂。

李四光的住所暂时被安排在六国饭店。约一星期后，搬到了北京饭店。第二天上午，李四光接到电话，问他下午是否外出，有人要来看他。黄昏时刻，客人来到了，李四光没想到来的竟是敬仰已久的周恩来总理。周总理与李四光畅谈了两三个小时。希望李四光除了在中国科学院协助郭沫若做好自然科学方面的工作外，还要把组织全国地质工作者为国家建设服务的主要责任担负起来。他们还互相交换了如何组织地质工作机构的初步设想。周总理的关怀和重视，给李四光这位在旧中国含辛茹苦地度过了大半生的科学家增添了巨大的力量。他曾经兴奋地说："今天是中国未有的大时代，一切人都要努力，不能落伍。"

1952年李四光与周恩来交谈。

1953年李四光与朱德在北戴河观察地质构造。

李四光到达北京不久，就赶上参加中国人民政治协商会议第一届全国委员会第二次会议。同时召开的还有全国高等教育会议和中国科学院第一次院务扩大会议，也都邀请他参加。6月16日，在全国政协会议上，周恩来总理做了政治报告。报告中提到李四光前不久曾向他谈到的西欧资本主义国家的某些情况，会议秘书处希望李四光在大会上也讲一讲。李四光在十来分钟的发言中，就在欧洲的所见所闻，分析了战后陷入困境的西欧资本主义国家，特别是老牌的英国和后起的美国之间的矛盾，就是“大帝国主义者要吃小帝国

主义者”。他说，美国是个大帝国主义者，“他们是要吃西欧的，什么大西洋联盟，欧洲经济复兴计划，马歇尔援欧计划等等，都是美帝要吃西欧的步骤。西欧各国为了要维持他们垂危的生命，一方面不得不向美帝乞怜，而另一方面又不得不设法抗拒，同时他们彼此又不能避免互相倾轧。他们的主要困难就在这里，而美帝控制西欧的策略，也要从这里找出来。”他还从资本主义的特性分析了西欧这些国家的统治阶级对新中国的矛盾态度。说明了当时英国政府既想承认我国，又怕得罪美国；既不愿平等对待我国，又想先进入中国市场的尴尬局面。在全国高教会议期间，李四光和其他代表一起受到毛泽东主席的接见。毛主席问候和赞扬了李四光，说：“李四光先生，你回来了，欢迎你。你在政协会上的发言讲得很好！”这次会见虽然时间很短，李四光却为毛主席的诚挚、谦逊和鼓励所深深感动。

李四光的中国科学院院士证书。

1954年初冬为中国科学院在北京郊区选址。左起：李四光、竺可桢、张稼夫、佚名、郭沫若、钱三强。

1956年李四光与刘少奇交谈。

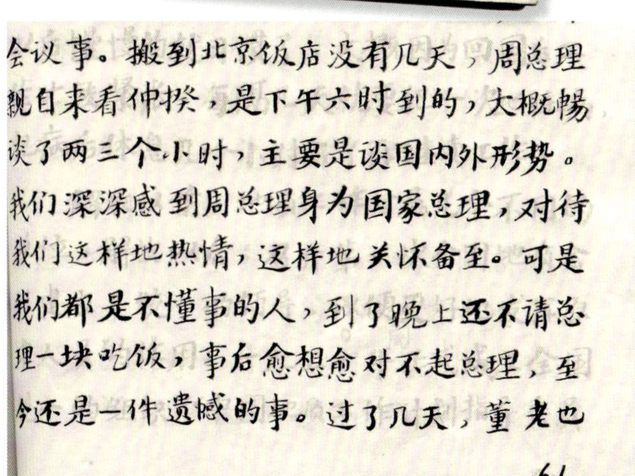

会议事。搬到北京饭店没有几天，周总理
亲自来看仲揆，是下午六时到的，大概畅
谈了两三个小时，主要是谈国内外形势。
我们深深感到周总理身为国家总理，对待
我们这样地热情，这样地关怀备至。可是
我们都是不懂事的人，到了晚上还不请总
理一块吃饭，事后愈想愈对不起总理，至
今还是一件遗憾的事。过了几天，董老也

61

在李夫人许淑彬的回忆录《回忆仲揆》中记载：1950年5月的一个下午，周恩来总理到当时他们暂住的北京饭店看望李四光。周恩来和李四光畅谈了两三个小时。

8月，中华全国第一次自然科学工作者代表大会在北京召开。在会上，周恩来总理做了《建设与团结》的报告。李四光以中国科学院副院长的身份做了《新中国的科学研究》的报告。严济慈代表大会筹备委员会常委会做了《一年来工作总结》的报告。在这次大会上，李四光被推选为中华全国自然科学专门学会联合会（简称科联）主席，侯德榜等为副主席。梁希被推选为中华全国科学技术普及协会（简称科协）主席，茅以升等为副主席。1951年4月，李四光还被推选为世界科学工作者协会执行委员会副主席。

1956年4月在北京参加科学工作者协会成立十周年大会，4月4日在会上发言。

1956年4月出席在北京召开的世界科协第16届执行局会议和世界科协成立十周年纪念大会，会议期间李四光和国际友人亲切交谈。

自从在北京饭店和周恩来总理谈话之后，李四光开始思考周总理交托的“组织全国地质工作者的任务”这个问题。旧中国有三个全国性的地质机构：中央地质调查所、中央研究院地质研究所、矿产测勘处，都设在南京。南京解放前夕，国民党政府南逃。这些机构的人员，在解放战争胜利形势的鼓舞下，都不愿跟国民党走。他们分别组织起来，坚持到南京解放，使这三个单位的图书资料、仪器设备基本完整地保存下来。但是，旧中国留下来的地质人员很少，新中国建设的地质工作任务很重，必须首先把全部力量放在配合国家经济建设上来。这一点，李四光在思想上是很明确的。问题是如何把地质界引导到这方面来，又如何把大家组织起来。为了广泛征求地质工作人员的意见，他亲自拟定了一封信，于5月中旬陆续发出，约发了200封，到8月陆续收到大部分回信。

经李四光综合考虑，并同有关方面协商，提出成立“一会、二所、一局”的意见：一会，即中国地质工作计划调配委员会，属政务院财政经济委员会和文化教育委员会领导；二所，即中国科学院地质研究所和古生物研究所；一局，即财政经济委员会矿产地质勘探局。8月，周总理主持召开的政务院第47次政务会议，通过了这个方案。在政务院通过时，将“中国地质工作计划调配委员会”改为“中国地质工作计划指导委员会”，同时任命李四光为主任委员，尹赞勋、谢家荣为副主任委员。

11月，李四光主持召开地质工作计划指导委员会扩大会议。到会的有委员、中央及大区地质机构的主要负责人、各大学地质系的主任教授和地质工作代表，共60余人。这是全国地质工作实行统一领导之后召开的第一次重要会议，也是地质界大团结的会议。会议认真讨论了“1951年工作计划大纲”“中央与地方机构的联系”等问题，并取得了一致的意见。

1956年4月出席在北京召开的世界科协第16届执行局会议和世界科协成立十周年纪念大会，会议期间李四光和科学院院长郭沫若一起会见国际友人。

1952年春李四光和夫人、女儿在遂安伯胡同家大门外。

1950年的年底，李四光迁到北京东城遂安伯胡同居住。

1954年在北京东城遂安伯胡同家大门前。

1953年秋李四光在遂安伯胡同家中抱着外孙女晒太阳。

1954年秋李四光在遂安伯胡同家中门前和外孙女一起玩。

1954年秋李四光夫妇与外孙女在院子里享受秋日阳光。

1954年冬李四光和夫人、女儿带着外孙女逛
北京北海公园。

1951年，全国开始进行大专院校的部分院系调整工作，经高教部和地质工作计划指导委员会共同商议，在北京大学、清华大学地质系及有关学系的基础上，扩大建立了北京地质学院，李四光亲自兼任北京地质学院筹备委员会主任。在东北各有关院系的基础上，加上原中央研究院一部分地质工作人员，扩大建立了长春地质学院。随后，又在南京大学、重庆大学等六个大学地质系中增设了专科班，还筹办了九个中等地质技术学校，设有钻探、化验、测绘等专业。所有这些，都为全面开展地质勘探工作培训技术干部，做好了准备。

1951年10月，李四光（第二排左二）与北京大学地质学系二年级全体学生合影。

20世纪50年代初李四光和北京大学地质学系学生交谈。

1954年李四光为中华人民共和国地质部揭牌。

随着国家经济建设有计划地大规模地开展，地质工作需要先行的任务越来越重，地质工作计划指导委员会的组织形式已经不能适应形势的需要。1952年8月，中央人民政府委员会第17次会议通过，决定成立地质部，李四光被任命为部长。同时派中央重工业部副部长、老红军何长工担任副部长。当时担任副部长的，还有刘杰（党组书记）和宋应。当周恩来总理派人事先和李四光商量建立地质部的有关事宜时，李四光非常高兴，感到这是中央对地质工作的关怀和重视，也是加强地质工作领导以适应国家经济建设需要的必要措施。11月下旬至12月初，地质部召开了全国地质工作计划会议。政务院副总理兼财政经济委员会主任陈云到会讲了话，强调从前地质工作是做多少算多少，国家没有整体计划，现在不同了，地质工作要根据国家建设的需要，目前更应根据钢铁工业、有色金属工业和燃料工业等建设的需要，在一定时间内探明一定的储量，地质事业在国家经济建设中已成了一项最重要的事业了。

地质部成立之后，国家逐年给地质部门调配了大批干部，加上各院校培养输送的专业人员和经过培训的工人，到第一个五年计划末，全国地质队伍已发展到20多万人。其中，受到高等教育的地质工作者，等于新中国成立前的60倍。探明的矿种和等级以及远景矿产储量，大大地增加了。新中国成立前全国仅对18种矿产做过调查，而且并未探明储量，到第一个五年计划末，地质部门已对71种矿产进行了勘探，其中有64种取得了储量。

1954年李四光在地质部院内。

20世纪50年代李四光和苏联专家在地质部门前。

1951年7月1日，是中国共产党诞生30周年纪念日。李四光出席了在北京隆重举行的庆祝大会，并以全国科联主席的身份发表献词。这是李四光第一次参加党的生日的活动。他满怀激情地谈了他站到革命队伍行列中后得到的一点新的认识。他说，30年，在我们中国的历史中，在世界无产阶级革命斗争的历史中，不算太长，就在这短促的时间内，却完成了空前伟大的事业。“2000多年的封建社会，已经被打垮了；100多年来，在中国肆行无忌的帝国主义以及和它勾结的一切恶势力，已经基本地被铲除了；以蒋介石为首的国民党反动政权被推翻了。差不多占全世界四分之一的人民，从黑暗的世

1953年李四光在北戴河考察地质。

界中，已经走进了光明的路上了。”他说：“为什么自从辛亥以来，中国人民要求革命，几次达到高潮，而终归失败？为什么在毛主席领导下，我们才有今日？”答案就是“把马列主义与中国的实际结合起来”。由此，他向全国科学工作者提出了努力学习马列主义、毛泽东思想，用辩证唯物主义来指导科研工作的任务。他认为，这种学习应该是理论联系实际的。“学习了之后，有时值得自己问一问，我们所了解的那些，究竟有多少仍然是属于书本上的教条，有多少已经形成了我们工作和思想的一部分？”

1954年李四光在北戴河考察地质。

1956年春李四光在北京香山附近考察地质。

李四光是一位自然科学家，他的科学成就，是和他在科学研究工作中重视哲学思维的修养、重视自然辩证法的学习和研究分不开的。在英国休养时，他已经在阅读恩格斯的《自然辩证法》。回国之后，他又读了毛泽东主席的《实践论》《矛盾论》等著作。并且提出“我们能不能善于把《实践论》《矛盾论》中所包含的一般真理，沿着我们地质工作者特殊的实践道路，由浅入深，一点一点地体现出来呢？这还是一个问题。但是，如果我们能这样做，那么不仅能引导我们胜利地去完成我们面临的迫切任务，而且引导我们的地质科学走向新的、更伟大的发展。”他还同有关部门商量，主张开展自然辩证法的研究，建立自然辩证法研究会。

李四光一面注意学习理论，一面注意自己的思想改造。而思想改造，正是通过学习马列主义、毛泽东思想的理论，自觉地开展批评和自我批评的方法进行的。在1952年的思想改造运动中，李四光更进一步体会到什么是真正的解放。他说：“大家以为把社会上破破烂烂的打碎，便是解放了；事实上那还不够，真正的战场，不在别处，而在我们自己的思想中。”“思想解放了，那才是真解放。”他先后在全国政协和中国科学院召开的会议上发言，以《一点初浅的认识》为题，谈自己思想的过去和现在。

关于中国石油资源的远景，在20世纪50年代以前，不少地质学家抱着悲观的看法。1915—1917年，美孚石油公司的一个钻井队，在陕北肤施（旧县名，于1937年并入延安县）一带，打了七口探井，花了300万美元，因收获不大走掉了。1922年，美国斯坦福大学教授布莱克·威尔德来中国调查地质，回去写了《中国和西伯利亚的石油资源》一文，发表在《美国矿冶工程师学会会报》上，提出了“中国贫油”的论点。他的文章归纳了三个原因，大意是：中国的中新生代缺乏海相沉积；古生界又是不含油的类型；除西藏、西北某些地区外，各时代地层都遭受了强烈的褶皱、断裂以及火成岩的侵入。于是他断言：“中国东南部找到石油的可能性不大；西南部找到石油的可能性更是遥远；西北部不会成为一个重要的油田；东北地区不会有大量的石油。”从此，“中国贫油”论就流传开来。

但是，李四光根据他对中国地质的深入研究，对“中国贫油”论一直持反对的态度。早在1928年，他在《燃料的问题》一文中指出：“美孚的失败，并不能证明中国没有油田可办。中国西北方出油的希望虽然最大，然而还有许多地方并非没有希望。热河据说也有油苗，四川的大平原也值得好好地研究，和四川赤盆地质上类似的地域也不少，都值得一番考察。”1935年，李四光在英国讲学期间，又暗示在我国东部有可能找到石油。他在《中国地质学》一书中，分析了新华夏构造体系沉降带发育的特点后指出：“这个新华夏系的内陆沉降带，我们有证据认为是白垩纪内陆盆地的发展。如

1955年8月李四光在大连疗养期间到大连白云山庄考察莲花状构造。

果在华北平原下部，钻探到足够的深度，似乎没有多大问题会遇到白垩纪地层，并且用地震的方法进行勘测时，可能揭露有重要经济价值的沉积物。”这里指的就是石油。

1953年，是我国第一个五年计划的头一年。这年的年底，毛泽东主席、周恩来总理和其他中央领导同志把李四光请到中南海，征询他对我国石油资源的看法。毛主席十分担心地对李四光说：“要进行建设，石油是不可缺少的，天上飞的，地下跑的，没有石油都转不动。”李四光根据数十年来对地质力学的研究，从他所建立的构造体系特别是新华夏构造体系的观点，分析了我国的地质条件，陈述了他不同意“中国贫油”论，深信在我国辽阔的领域内，天然石油资源的蕴藏量应当是丰富的，关键是要抓紧做地质勘探工作。他提出应当打开局限于西北一隅的石油勘探局面，在全国范围内广泛开展石油地质普查工作，找出几个希望大、面积广的可能含油地区。中央领导同志赞成李四光的这些意见，后来周总理在国务院司局长干部会议上做报告时提到了这件事，他说：“石油在我们的工业中是最薄弱的一个环节，……首先是勘探的情况不明。地质部部长很乐观，对我们说，地下蕴藏量很大，很有希望。我们很拥护他的意见。”

在我国辽阔的领域内，如何选定可能的含油地区，对我国石油普查勘探具有重大的战略意义。油区是生油和储油条件比较优越的地区，而油田是储油条件特别好的地区。李四光从构造地质角度出发，认为找油要先找油区，再找油田。选定油区的地质条件，李四光认为应该考虑：一、在沉积岩层厚度大，岩相不单一，有机物质多，挽近地质时代长期下沉而且幅度较大，对生油、储油有利的地区；二、在褶皱不强烈，有扭动运动和旋扭运动造成的构造，对油气集中有利的地区；三、储油岩层和它形成的构造埋伏在较浅的地下，对油气保存有利的地区；四、在我国首先着重中生代、新生代地层分布的地区。李四光认为具备或基本具备这四个条件的地区，大都位于一定类型的巨型构造体系的沉降部位，即一个可能含油的广大地区的展布范围，是

1957年夏李四光在青岛疗养院住所门前和女儿、女婿、外孙女及女婿的朋友合影。

1957年夏李四光和家人在青岛疗养院住所房前草地上。

被有关巨型构造体系所控制着。而在这样的地区，要找到油田也应该先寻找储油构造，找到构造之后再搞地层。如果把“目的层”当成找油的重点，这不是多快好省的办法。因为油是活动的，运动很复杂，它要适应种种地质构造条件和构造岩石条件。在绝大多数的场合，生油地区不一定是储油地区，反过来也是这样。当然生油问题可以探讨，但对勘探来讲是次要的，而找构造是主要的。找油的关键是在于对构造的正确认识。

1954年初，苏联派来了一个石油代表团帮助我国找油。他们在中国西北、西南等地看了之后，回到北京，提出希望听听李四光的意见。同年2月，李四光应邀到石油管理总局做了题为《从大地构造看我国石油勘探的远景》的报告。

李四光说：“我认为提出下面两点，对我们的石油勘探工作有很大关系，一是关于沉积的条件，二是关于地质构造的条件。这两点不是孤立的，当然是有联系的。”他对这两点作了概略的说明之后，接着指出了我国石油勘探远景最大的区域有以下三个：“一、青、康、滇、缅大地槽；二、阿拉善—陕北盆地；三、东北平原—华北平原。”他说：当然这并不是说“除了这几个区域外，别处就可以不做工作了”。接着，李四光详细地分析了这三大含油远景区域的地质构造特点和应该研究的问题，并且提出了应该首先把柴达木盆地、黑河地区、四川盆地、伊陕台地、阿宁台地、华北平原、东北平原等地区，作为寻找石油的对象。他还明确指出：新华夏系的构造带，其主要走向为北18度至东25度，包括太平洋岛弧在内。这里所说的是第一级的大地构造，有比较长期的发展历史，其主要凹陷带对储存石油具有比较好的条件。他说：“可以这样考虑：从东北平原起，通过渤海湾，到华北平原，再往南到两湖地区，可以做工作，先从新华夏系的旁边摸起；同时在覆盖地区着手摸底，物探、钻探都可以上，看来是有重要意义的。”李四光的报告长达一天，给我国石油工作者以很大的鼓舞。

9月，李四光出席第一届全国人民代表大会，并就五年来地质工作取得的成就和存在的问题，做了发言。根据会议决定，他连任地质部部长。12月，在全国政协二届一次会议上，李四光当选为副主席。

为了迅速扭转石油普查勘探工作的落后局面，国务院决定，从1955年起，除由燃料工业部石油管理总局继续加强对可能含油构造的细测和钻探外，并由地质部、中国科学

1957年夏李四光和夫人、外孙女在青岛疗养院住所门前。

院分别担任石油和天然气的普查工作和科学研究工作。1956年3月，由地质部、石油工业部、中国科学院联合成立了以李四光为主任委员的全国石油地质委员会，作为全国石油地质的咨询机构。

1955年1月，地质部召开第一次全国石油普查工作会议。李四光致开幕词。许杰副部长做了《关于1955年石油、天然气普查工作的方针与任务》的报告。会议结束前夕，李四光主持部务会议，批准了会议决议。根据这个决议，地质部组建了新疆、柴达木、鄂尔多斯、四川、华北五个石油普查大队。6月，又决定组织松辽平原踏勘组。这一年是全国石油地质普查工作大丰收的一年，发现了很多可能储油的构造，同时通过对华北平原、松辽平原的概略普查，认为这两个地区具有较好的含油远景，值得进一步开展工作。

1956年1月，地质部召开第二次全国石油普查工作会议，总结1955年工作，布置1956年任务。会议决定：1956年将在12地区派遣93个地质队，包括430名地质工作人员，进行石油普查和部分详查细测。会议还听取了松辽踏勘组的报告，决定组成松辽石油普查大队和112物探队，开展全盆地的石油普查工作。

会议期间，陈云副总理找李四光谈话，详细地询问了石油地质普查的情况。根据陈云副总理的指示，李四光在同地质部和石油工业部领导同志交换了意见之后，于2月4日就如何在总结过去所获得的勘探成果的基础上，在选定的油区内迅速发现油田，从而对我国天然石油远景做出可靠的评价问题，向陈云副总理做了书面报告。

至此，地质部根据李四光的意见，在第一个五年计划的后三年，对石油地质开始在全国范围内做了战略的展开。十分明显，根据当时掌握的地质资料和地质队伍的有限力量，把工作重点放在了西北地区；同时组织适当力量开始了东部新区的找油工作。经过三年的石油普查工作，在新疆、青海、四川、江苏、贵州、广西及华北、东北等有希望的含油远景区，找到了几百个可能的储油构造。并在柴达木油砂山、冷湖、马海等构造上，探到了具有工业价值的油流。但是，到第二个五年计划开始的时候，还未能肯定一个产量很大的油田，石油资源仍然非常紧张。

1955年秋，李四光迁到北京西城嘉祥里胡同居住。第二年冬，因患肾脏病，住北京医院。1957年1月，到杭州疗养，住南山招待所。

1957年夏李四光在青岛疗养时的全家福。

1957年2月中旬李四光在杭州会见苏联地质保矿部部长安特罗波夫，会见后在南山招待所住所前合影。

1957年4月在杭州南山招待所疗养期间李四光和外孙女在住所门外享受春日阳光。

1957年春李四光夫妇在杭州疗养期间。

1957年春李四光在杭州和夫人、外孙女。

1957年3月李四光和夫人带着外孙女在杭州西湖边散步。

1957年6月李四光在杭州和外孙女一起在公园散步。

1957年7月在青岛海滩上李四光和
夫人、女婿、外孙女一起玩水。

1957年8月李四光和夫人在青岛带着外孙女郊游。

为了祖国的建设

The Spirit of Reconstruction (1957—1965)

李四光一生经历了一条漫长而曲折的道路，而在他进入古稀之年时，才找到了“归宿”，加入了中国共产党。正像他在党支部大会上说的那样，他“像是一个刚出生的婴儿，生命的新起点才开始”。从此，他感到生活是那么美好和充实，以70岁的高龄，奋斗在地质科学战线上，他恨不能把他全部的智慧和力量，都在一刻间倾倒出来，献给党，献给人民。

李四光要求入党，是1957年正式提出来的。他向党表达自己的这个夙愿也是经过了一番严峻思索的。早在20世纪50年代初，有人请李四光参加“中国国民党革命委员会”，后来还有人要他参加中国民主同盟和九三学社，他都婉言谢绝了。当时，李四光的心愿是想加入中国共产党，但就怕不够资格，不敢提出来。他常想，在共产党领导中国人民进行几十年艰苦卓绝的革

1958年6月摘除左肾手术后在颐和园介寿堂疗养期间李四光和女婿、外孙女在湖上荡舟。

1959年初夏李四光在北京西山象鼻子沟居所门前。

1958年9月李四光在北京西山象鼻子沟家中和前来参加全国第一次矿产会议的苏联代表团成员握手。

1958年9月李四光、地质力学所的研究人员和前来参观的苏联地质保矿部部长安特罗波夫和代表团其他成员在北京西山象鼻子沟地质力学研究所大楼外台阶上合影。

命武装斗争中，在无数先烈为共产主义理想抛头颅洒热血的年代里，自己没有这个觉悟，没有投身于革命队伍中，内心感到非常惭愧；现在共产党领导人民夺取了政权，成了执政的党，在这个时候提出要求入党，他认为当然是不够资格的。同时他也感到，自己虽然对党有了一定的认识，但从阶级觉悟和世界观的改造来讲，还只是刚刚开始，离一个中国共产党党员的标准，还有一段很大的距离，特别是在对党的事业的贡献上，自己还没做什么事。再加上自己年龄大了，身体又不好，入了党是否能起一个中国共产党党员的作用，也是一个问题。

1957年3月的一天，李四光因病在杭州疗养，突然听到外面有人说："周总理来了。"李四光夫妇还没有来得及穿上外衣，周恩来总理已经来到会客室的门口。李四光激动地握着周总理的手，把周总理迎了进来。周总理坐在沙发上，首先问起李四光的身体和病情，接着又和李夫人谈了一会儿家常。李夫人离开后，周总理和李四光又谈了很久。就在这次会见中，周总理问起李四

1958年9月李四光在北京西山象鼻子沟地质力学研究所与前来参加全国第一次矿产会议的苏联地质保矿部部长安特罗波夫。

1959年4月李四光在野外鉴定冰溜擦痕。

李四光的手电筒和看书用的放大镜。

1959年夏李四光在北京西山八大处考察冰川擦痕。

光对加入中国共产党的想法。李四光望着周恩来总理亲切、热情的目光，听着他诚恳、晓畅的谈话，心中充满着温暖之情。他向周总理诉说了自己要求加入中国共产党的心愿以及为什么考虑多年而又没有提出来的原因。针对李四光的思想，周总理耐心地做了工作。周总理的这次谈话，使李四光在前进的道路上增添了勇气。他决心不辜负周总理的殷切期望，把自己的余生，毫无保留地贡献给党，贡献给壮丽的共产主义事业。

6月，李四光在人民日报上发表了文章《党能领导科学工作》。这是李四光运用马列主义、毛泽东思想，具体地分析和解决党如何正确地领导科学工作问题的一篇重要文章。据他的了解，党对科学工作的领导作用，起码有两点：第一，“保证科学研究工作服务于社会主义建设的需要”，包括“目前迫切的需要和长远的需要”。李四光认为，“只有党才能全面了解我国社会主义各方面的需要，也只有党才能领导这样巨大而繁杂的组织工作”。第二，保证科学研究工作在辩证唯物主义世界观的指导下进行。李四光认为，科学愈发展，分工愈细致。一方面，“科学家在他的专业范围内能提

1959年夏李四光夫妇和外孙女在西山象鼻子沟居所门前。

1959年11月李四光陪同苏联地质学家纳里夫金院士等到北京西山察看冰川遗迹，休息时合影。

出最好的意见。正因为如此，每个科学家也就很容易倾向于强调本行的业务”。另一方面，“实际问题的处理，却常常要求许多科学部门彼此联系和协作，也就是说要求以辩证唯物的观点来看问题”。“辩证唯物主义世界观就是共产主义世界观。我们迫切需要党从这个方面来领导我们。”他说：“这就要求负责领导工作的党员同志，更好地提高他们的辩证唯物主义水平。同时我也觉得，除此而外，最好这些同志们还能抽出些时间多学习些科学业务，而科学家也能抽些时间多学习些马列主义。双方从思想上到具体工作上都能有共同语言，也就能结合得更好些。”文章最后写道：“就一个世纪以来，尤其是近几十年来的历史经验教训来说，只有共产党在中国政治历史上出现以后，中国人民才找到正确的领导，脱离了受屈辱、受压迫的生活，并且在全世界面前站起来了。像我们这样一个经济落后的大国，在贪得无厌的国际帝国主义面前，要迅速地富强起来，除了走社会主义道路以外，

肯定是没有其他路可走的。要走社会主义的路，除了实行人民民主专政，也肯定是没有其他政治路线可循的。要实行人民民主专政，建设社会主义，没有共产党来领导，肯定是不行的。”

这期间，中国科学院党组派代表到杭州来探望李四光。李四光又就当前科学工作的几个重大问题坦率地谈了自己的意见。在谈到科学体制问题时，他说：“根据我国科学研究的落后状况，集中力量加强科学院，很有必要。当然，如果学校有力量，也应该搞些科学研究，特别是缺门科学，科学院要搞，学校也可以搞。”在谈到理论与实际统一的原则问题时，他说：“我们的科学发展主要是为国家建设服务，目前国家建设中的问题，如不能得到解决，国家就站不起来。但是，解放后批评脱离实际这个问题时，有过火之处，有命令主义，甚至加以压力。有的人怕说不联系实际，连显微镜也不敢看了。向科学进军以来，又有另一种倾向，有些人想丢开实际工作去搞大而空的理论。有些青年人产生了做研究生有前途，做技术员没有前途的想法。这是一个重要问

1959年11月李四光陪同苏联地质学家纳里夫金院士等到北京西山察看冰川遗迹。

题，如何纠正一下才好。”在谈到百家争鸣问题时，他说：“从科学方面来说，鸣不鸣要以有无实际问题为基础，这样就会切实些。光讲空论，花去不少时间，得不到结果。同时，我们应该鼓励青年人，特别是让那些有造诣、态度谦虚、工作达到一定水平的青年人也敢于发表意见，参加到争鸣的队伍中来。这样也会显得有个新气象。不然老是几个老人来透老气，当然让他们透透老气也好，但都是老气看不出新气也不好。青年人队伍大，吸收一些青年人参加进来，使空气新鲜、愉快些。”在谈到党对科学工作的领导问题

1959年11月李四光为新成立的地质力学研究所题写所名，并亲自设计用大理石雕刻制作。

1953年李四光和在秦皇岛野外实习的北京地质学院学生交谈。

20世纪60年代初李四光参加学习会。

时，他说："今后应该注意，不要用运动的形式来搞科学。比如，说发展科学，就全面搞开；说收缩，一切都停止；说改善条件，什么都要买新的；说节约，一切又停下来。这些都是运动的方式。"他还说：科学工作也像中国革命一样，"没有党的领导不成"。但是，党的领导"不能光讲是搞后勤的"。"科学问题虽然由科学家去搞，而发动和组织科学家进行百花齐放、百家争鸣的力量，没有党不成，不然就会发生混乱，陷于没有步骤，与国家方向背道而驰，弄得不团结，情况不堪设想。"

地质部党组也派代表到杭州来探望李四光。他们就地质工作应怎样加强领导问题，广泛地交换了意见。李四光首先指出，当前地质工作存在的主要问题，"是计划性不强，计划变更多，干部调动频繁"，同时，对实际情况的了解工作也做得不够，包括投入力量的区域的实际情况和干部力量的实际情况。他说："地质部作为一个政府部门，任务是很明确的，最后还是要搞出储量，搞清矿种在区域上与深度方面的分布。"要解决这些问题，第一步是地面测量，第二步是深处勘测，这两步是配合的。"勘探设计工作，应慎重考虑。要注意当地的地貌、地文等条件。如果简单地布置网、槽，就会引起浪费。"他说，搞地质工作计划，首先要考虑的是区域的选择。"要根据矿种的要求，选择最有希望的地区，这样力量可以比较集中些，并要同其他

20世纪60年代初李四光在地质部院内。

单位采取协作的方针”；其次，“要选择若干关键性的问题，即对找矿起着主要作用的，来从事研究工作”，这就不能限于哪一个区域，有的甚至可以追到国外；再次，“同其他部门的分工问题，要通过国务院去协调”。

在这短短的一段时间里，李四光接连三次发表谈话，中心内容是围绕着党如何加强对科学工作和地质工作的领导问题，既肯定了成绩，又指出了缺点，还提出了改进的措施，意见是那样的尖锐和中肯。这反映了李四光对事物的洞察力和思想水平。

1957年7月，李四光从杭州转青岛疗养。9月，李四光的肾脏病加重，发现小便带血，背部生疔。经青岛疗养院X光检查，左肾有一个圆形的阴影，认为有肿瘤的嫌疑，建议做进一步鉴定。同北京联系后，请来了内科和泌尿科专家，认为应速返京会诊，进行手术治疗。这时，李四光的心情不禁有些紧张，这么大年纪了，还要挨一刀，是否值得呢？他要求向周恩来总理汇报，请示意见。

11月，李四光从青岛回到北京，住北京医院，继续观察。在住院期间，周总理先后三次前来探望。第一次，是李四光住院不久。那天，周总理披着医院的一件白大褂，笑呵呵地走进门来，坐在李四光的病床旁边，详细地询问了李四光的身体情况，并安慰他安心治病，接着又高兴地谈起了家常，讲了许多有趣的事情。第二次，是李四光动手术的前一天，周总理又来到医院，亲自审阅了手术方案，询问了手术中可能发生的情况及处理方法，最后批准了这次手术。还到李四光的病房，坐了约有15分钟，给李四光带来了战胜疾病的勇气和力量。在周总理的亲切关怀和医务人员的努力下，手术顺利地做完了。最后证实，李四光患的不是肿瘤，而是肾结石把左肾磨了个大水泡，但因病情在发展，整个左肾还是被切掉了。手术后，李四光身体十分虚弱。这时，周总理第三次来到医院探望，要李四光安心养病，以便尽快恢复健康，好为人民服务。周总理这样无微不至的关怀，使李四光永志不忘。

经过一个多月的治疗，李四光手术后的刀口基本上愈合了，但创痛还没有完全消除。医院这个小天地，对李四光来说，实在是住不惯，他急于要求出院，医院没有办法，只好同意。12月，李四光来到庭院深深的颐和园介寿堂疗养。

1958年6月，李四光转到青岛太平角疗养。在医务人员的精心护理之下，李四光的健康逐渐恢复，紧张的工作随之也开始了。

8月，中国科学院成立原子能委员会，李四光被任命为主任委员。

9月，全国第一届矿产会议开幕。李四光主持了这次会议，并在会上致了开幕词。会议的主要目的，是总结和交流新中国成立以来我国地质矿产普查和勘探的经验。

中国科学技术协会在北京成立。这个新的全国性的科学技术团体，是由中华全国自然科学专门学会联合会和中华全国科学技术普及协会合并组成的。大会选出了149人的全国委员会作为中国科学技术协会的领导机构。全国委员会选举李四光为中国科学技术协会主席。

1960年夏李四光在北京西山考察地质。

1960年李四光与地质部党组书记何长工在西山象鼻子沟住处院外。

10月18日，李四光开始填写入党志愿书。他严肃地用工整的钢笔字写下了下面这一段话：“几年来，我看见不少的老朋友和许多青年同志，都努力改造自己，力求进步，终于能够像婴儿投入母亲的怀抱那样，投入了党的怀抱。”“如果我也能够最后光荣地参加党的大家庭，我相信一定有更多的机会得到同志们更多的帮助。我自己决心以‘活到老，学到老’的精神来改造自己，使我这个个体能够更好地在党的领导下，为祖国的社会主义、共产主义建设服务，为中国人民服务。”李四光的入党介绍人是地质部党组书记何长工和中国科学院党组书记张劲夫。

12月22日，中共地质部办公厅第一支部召开支部大会，讨论了李四光的入党申请。李四光在会上做了两次发言。他说：“我们这一辈人的时代，是一个了不得的时代。它的特点就是变，全世界翻天覆地的变。回忆清朝末年，封建王朝的统治，腐败到了极点。甲午之战被日本打败，庚子之战又受八国联军的蹂躏。它的软弱无能，完全暴露，形势是危急的。”“我也和全国部分青年一样，投入了辛亥革命的战斗。辛亥革命以后，清朝的统治不存在了，名义上的共和国建立起来了，但是旧势力依然占着统治的地位。”“在这个时候，我也和一部分参加过辛亥革命的人们一样，认为革命要继续下去是肯定的，但是在进行革命斗争的道路上，由于针对的目标不同，当时发觉有两个不同的途径：其一，针对着国内的反动势力，就应该在国内用一切方法和它作你死我活的斗争，达到彻底铲除旧的反动势力，重新建立真正的民主共和。其二，针对着国内反动派的后台老板——帝国主义，就要做长期打算，趁着年轻有为的时候，去到欧洲继续进修学技术，企图学会一套本领，来对抗帝国主义对我们的侵略、压迫和剥削。我选择了后一途径。”李四光接着说：“在最初选择从事科学研究的途径的时候，满以为只要稍有理智的人，都要在真理的面前低头。但是，在北洋军阀及国民党反动集团统治的时期，根本没有真理可言。到了（20世纪）30年代，特别是西安事变以后，也是许多高级知识分子纷纷向往庐山召见的时候，由于那种刻骨的刺激，我才开始深深感到，只有在中国共产党的旗帜下，把饱受压迫和剥削的广大工农群众团结起来，才能保证走向革命的胜利。当时，我一面痛恨那个反动统治集团，感到和它不共戴天，但同时又舍不得放弃科学研究，特别是想揭穿地壳构成的规律和它形成过程的谜。现在，我们的大陆解放了。一个落后的国家，蜕变而为强大的中华人民共和国，像磐石一样屹立在地球上。我们这些为数不多的地质工作者，各自在黑暗中摸索前进的痛苦阶段，从此结束了。”李四光的发言结束以后，大家相继发言。李四光对同志们提出的意见，在本子上认真地记录下来，态度很严肃。接着，支部大会一致通过了接收李四光为中共预备党员。随后，地质部机关党委和中央国家机关党委先后批复同意支部的决议。1960年6月，经中央组织部、中央国家机关党委批准，李四光按期转为中共正式党员。从此，李四光在理想和信念的境界上，跨上了一个新高度。

这一年秋，李四光迁到北京西山象鼻子沟居住。

1960年夏李四光夫妇在北京西山象鼻子沟通往地质力学研究所的小路上和地质部领导在一起。前排左二起：何长工、李四光、许淑彬。后排右二：肖赤。

1959年，是中华人民共和国成立十周年，也是李四光入党后的头一年。他曾对一位外国朋友说："我个人能够生逢这样伟大的时代，我深深感到生活真有意义，生命值得珍贵。"他似乎突然变得年轻了，浑身好像蕴藏着使不完的力量。然而，究竟已是古稀之年，又有病魔缠身，领导上特别关心他的健康，医生也嘱咐他要注意休息。对此，李四光是十分感激的。但他在自己的心中，却早已另有一番考虑和安排。

早在20世纪40年代中叶，李四光曾撰写过《地质力学的基础与方法》一书，此书虽然也是一次总结性的文献，但那仅仅是地质力学诞生时期具备的一个雏形。新中国成立后，李四光又发表了一系列有关地质力学方面的著

1960年夏李四光夫妇与肖赤、何长工夫人等在象鼻子沟后山坡上。

作，如1951年的《受了歪曲的亚洲大陆》，1953年的《地质构造的三重基本概念》，1954年的《旋卷构造及其他有关中国西北部大地构造体系复合问题》，1955年的《地壳运动问题》（讨论提纲），1957年的《莲花状构造》，1959年的《东西复杂构造带和南北构造带》，等等，大大丰富和发展了地质力学的内容。此外，有些国外学者也从不同角度或者从某一方面开展了地质力学的研究。李四光认为，这些都需要进行系统的总结。

1959年1月，李四光在青岛疗养时，开始了《地质力学概论》的写作。李四光从自己著述的经验中，深知写一本科学著作，是需要耗费巨大的精力和大量的时间的。从他当时的身体情况和时间来看，必须采取一种快速而有效的形式，才能在较短的时期内，完成这篇著作。后来，李四光决定采取由他口述，由秘书记录，然后加以整理，再由他过目修改和补充的办法进行写作。在动手写作之前，李四光已对全书的章节和内容有了腹稿，因此，开始后进行得还是比较顺利的。这样，经过一个多月的努力，整理出来的文稿共五章，约八万字，总题目初定为《地质力学的方法与实践》。他把这个初稿带到北京打印后，请地质力学研究所的同志们进行了讨论，广泛听取群众的意见。大家提出了探讨性和建设性的意见，有170多条。根据大

1960年春在紫竹院公园和地质力学研究所研究人员在一起。
左起：杨怀仁、刘国昌、李四光、李承三、孙殿卿、景才瑞。

1961年秋李四光夫妇和女儿、女婿、外孙女在青岛疗养院住所外。

家的意见，李四光认为，这本书的内容有扩大的必要。现在是社会主义建设时期，急需的是寻找地下矿产资源和工程地质、水文地质等方面的应用。特别是在沉积矿产方面，如指出天然石油远景，这已经在生产实践中，部分地得到了检验。关于构造体系展布的规律和分级控矿理论，看来也是行之有效的。这方面的经验，必须总结进去。但是，李四光深知自己要在有生之年，全部总结出一个比较完整的梗概，是颇有问题的。他想，总的命题还是叫作《地质力学的方法与实践》，不妨把这次总结作为第一篇概论看待，第二篇可以考虑叫作构造体系分论或典型构造体系各论，第三篇就写岩石力学性质和构造应力场的分析，第四篇再阐明地壳运动问题。先把第一篇概论写好，第二篇、第三篇、第四篇留到以后再做。这样，在李四光的心里，就有了一部比较完整的、系统的总结计划。即使自己不能写成全书，只要有了大纲，留下的部分还可以由后人来完成。接着，李四光在初稿的基础上进行修改和补充。他把初稿的五章，调整为四章，即：第一章，有关地质构造的若干传统概念述要；第二章，地质力学的方法；第三章，当前地质力学中存在的问题；第四章，地质构造运动起源问题；但内容则增补了不少。第二次打印稿已扩充到13万多字了，在地质力学研究所又一次组织了讨论，时间长达一个

1961年夏李四光在青岛疗养院住所前和前来探望他的朋友合影。

月。这样，一直到1962年初，李四光终于完成了这部重要著作《地质力学概论》。可以说，这是李四光40年实践经验的总结，是他在地质力学方面的代表作，也是地质力学研究史中的一个里程碑。

1959年3月，李四光收到苏联一个发行很广的《自然》杂志主编谢尔巴柯夫的一封来信，恳切地约请李四光给他们写一篇有关中华人民共和国建国十年来地质工作发展的文稿。李四光对这件事十分重视。他认为新中国成立十周年大庆就要到来，这类文章如果带有浓厚的应节性气味，写出来乏味，但可以借此比较全面地回顾总结一下十年来地质工作的概况，看来也并不是毫无意义的。4月，李四光回信同意谢尔巴柯夫约稿的请求。信中说：“我初步考虑，拟以《建国十年来中国地质工作的发展》为题写一短文。我想这样的文章可能使苏联地质界的朋友们感到兴趣。尽管我的健康使我现时仍然在断断续续地养病，但我仍争取把它写成。”

李四光虽然是这么说，可是他一动笔，就十分认真地开始了写作。文章从起草到完稿，他反复修改了12次之多。李四光的这篇文章，比较系统地总结了构造带和构造体系控矿的理论，这是他对寻找矿产资源的独特贡献。他指出："国家工业建设不断地迅速发展，要求我们在已知的地质条件基础上，进行普查和进一步的勘探工作。最重要的已知地质条件，就是已知的重要矿区的分布，大都落在若干地带。那些地带是和第一级的重要构造带大体一致的。就是说，已知矿区的分布是受到几个第一级大构造带的控制。其中有些矿体和矿脉，是受到形成第一级构造的构造运动所产生的次一级和再次一级的构造体系的控制。""有的构造带是单独存在的，有的是与其他构造带交叉的，在交叉的地区，往往有矿区密集现象。"文章接着指出，受到第一级构造体系控制的大矿区，可以分为五个不同地带：一、围绕西藏高原及其邻近地区的隆起、凹陷和褶皱地带。包括中国部分的天山褶皱带、昆仑山褶皱带、祁连山褶皱带、青川滇南北向褶皱带及一些山间盆地，如准噶尔、塔里木、柴达木等盆地。在这些山岳褶皱地区，有着不同时期、不同类型的火成岩活动和多次运动所形成的构造带。这些构造带中，主要寻找各种金属矿床。在这个区域中的大小山间盆地，亦即湖相或海相地层中，寻找石油及其他有用盐类。二、中国东部和沿海地区的走向北北东—南南西的隆起、凹陷和褶皱地带。这个构造带被称为新华夏系构造带。在松辽平原、渤海湾和华北平原地带，正在进行石油勘探和普查工作，

20世纪50年代李四光在地质部领导会议上发言。

并在松辽平原的钻井中，发现了多层油砂的存在。这种发现对其他地区如渤海湾、华北平原乃至苏北平原的石油勘测工作，给予很大支持。三、阴山地带。这是个横亘东西的地带。东段从长白山起，往西经河北北部、内蒙古自治区、中国-蒙古边境一直到新疆。这个带多金属矿区出现比较频繁。四、秦岭地带。几年来我们在这一带的勘探工作，主要集中在它的中部及东部，亦即由陕西蓝田至河南伊阳地带。已找到的主要矿产有：除矽卡岩型铁矿及铜、铅、锌矿以外，还找到了巨大的细脉浸染型钼矿。在东部海州地区有磷灰岩矿床，产于结晶岩和杂岩中。五、南岭地带。包括赣南、湖南、粤北、广西东南部等地区。新中国成立以来，对各种金属矿产进行了比较广泛的普查与勘探，特别是对钨、锡矿及和它们共生的有色金属矿。在上述五个地带

1962年李四光（一排右五）、何长工（一排右四）会见地质力学研究所员工后合影。

中，特别是在三个复杂的东西构造带中，或多或少都发现了稀有和分散元素，因此在这方面的找矿工作虽然开始不久，但已找到了许多相当重要的矿床，展示了良好的前景。

1959年是李四光写作上丰收的一年，他一连写下了12篇著作。其中，除了《地质力学概论》《建国十年来中国地质工作的发展》以外，还有专门性的地质论文《东西复杂构造带和南北构造带》《地质学的现在和未来》以及为少年儿童阅读的科普文章《看看我们的地球》等，内容十分广泛。这是新中国成立以来，李四光写作最多的一个年头。

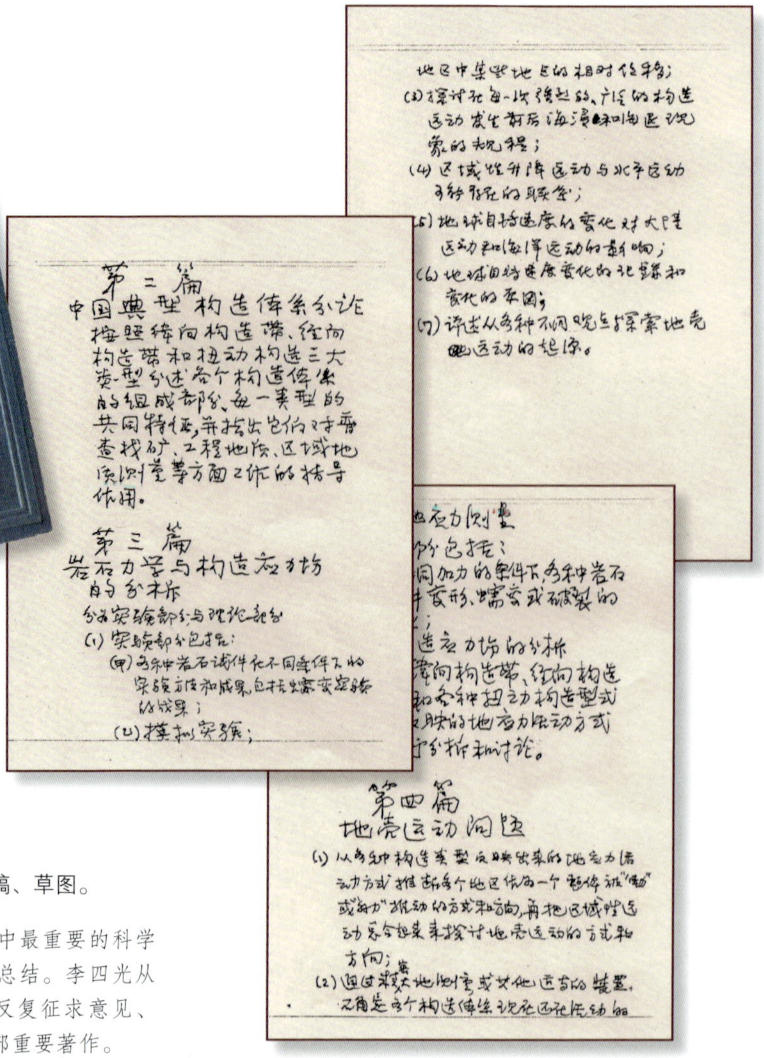

地区中某些地区的相对位移；
(3)探讨在每一次强烈的、广泛的构造运动发生前后海浸和海退现象的规程；
(4)区域性升降运动与水平运动可能存在的联系；
(5)地球自转速度的变化对大陆运动和海洋运动的影响；
(6)地球自转速度变化的记录和变化的原因；
(7)评述从各种不同观点探索地壳运动的起源。

第二篇
中国典型构造体系分论
按照纬向构造带、经向构造带和扭动构造三大类型分述各个构造体系的组成部分、每一类型的共同特征，并指出它们对于普查找矿、工程地质、区域地质测量等方面工作的指导作用。

第三篇
岩石力学与构造应力场的分析
分为实验部分与理论部分
(1)实验部分包括：
(甲)各种岩石试件在不同条件下的实验方法和成果，包括蠕变实验的成果；
(2)模拟实验；

第四篇
地壳运动问题
(1)从各种构造类型反映出来的地应力活动方式推断各个地区作为一个整体被"推"或"拖"挠动的方式和方向，再把区域性运动综合起来来探讨地壳运动的方式和方向；
(2)通过精密大地测量或其他适当的装置，确定各个构造体系现在还在活动的

《地质力学概论》封面及部分草稿、草图。

《地质力学概论》是李四光一生中最重要的科学专著之一，是他40年实践经验的总结。李四光从1959年1月开始写作，经过三年反复征求意见、修改，终于在1962年初完成了这部重要著作。

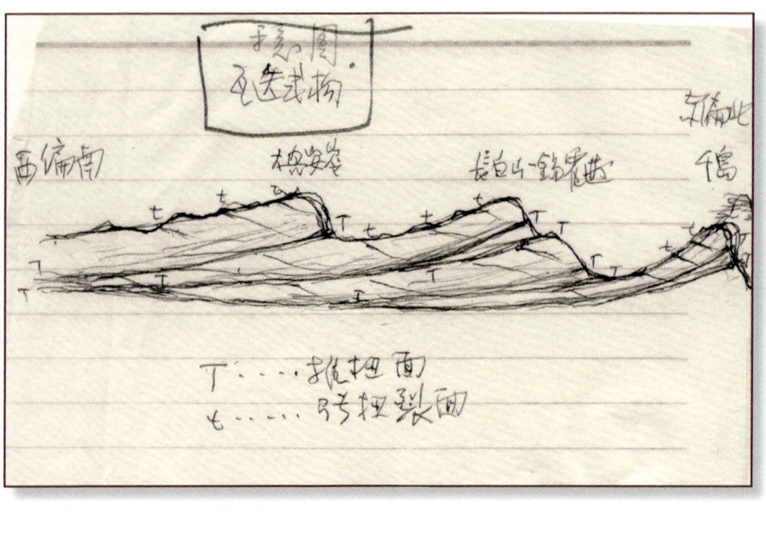

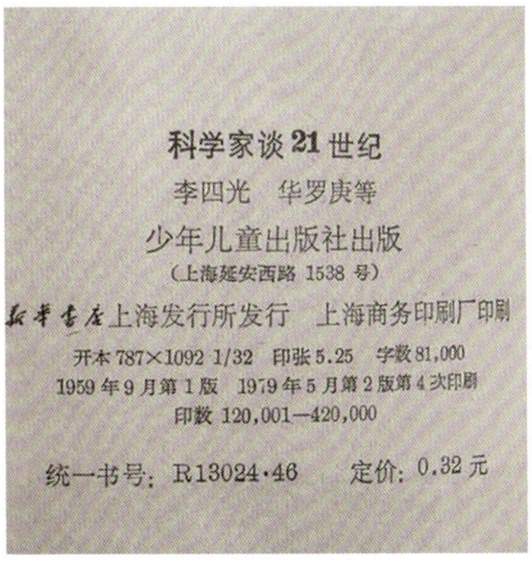

科学家谈21世纪

李四光　华罗庚等

少年儿童出版社出版

（上海延安西路1538号）

新华书店上海发行所发行　上海商务印刷厂印刷

开本787×1092 1/32　印张5.25　字数81,000

1959年9月第1版　1979年5月第2版第4次印刷

印数 120,001—420,000

统一书号：R13024·46　定价：0.32元

《科学家谈21世纪》封面及版权页。

1959年初李四光收到了上海少年儿童出版社的一封约稿信，为了写好这篇给孩子读的科普文章，他特意停了《地质力学概论》的写作，用了一周的时间写出了《看看我们的地球》。文章虽然只有3000多字，可是字字都经过他认真推敲，唯恐孩子们读不懂。

看看我们的地球*

地球是围绕太阳旋转的九大行星之一，它是一个离太阳不太远也不太近的第三个行星。它的周围有一圈大气，这圈大气组成它的最外一层，就是气圈。在这层下面，就是有些地方是由岩石造成的大陆，大致占地球总面积的十分之三，也就是石圈的表面。其余的十分之七都是海洋，称为水圈。水圈的底下，也都是石圈。不过，在大海底下的这一部分石圈的岩石，它的性质和大陆上露出的岩石的性质一般是不同的。大海底下的岩石重一些、黑一些，大陆上的岩石比较轻一些，一般颜色也淡一些。

石圈不是由不同性质的岩石规规矩矩造成的圈子，而是在地球出生和它存在的几十亿年的过程中，发生了多次的翻动，原来埋在深处的岩石，翻到地面上来了。这样我们才能直接看到曾经埋在地下深处的岩石，也才能使我们能

* 该文是李四光教授给少年儿童写的一篇科学小品。文章深入浅出地介绍了地球的结构和在太阳系中的位置，以及它的起源的不同学说，刊在《科学家谈二十一世纪》一书中，由上海少年儿童出版社出版，1959年10月。

64

看看我们的地球

够想象到石圈深处的岩石是什么样子。

随着科学不断地发达，人类对自然界的了解是越来越广泛和深入了，可是到现在为止，我们的眼睛所能钻进石圈的深度，顶多也还不过十几公里。而地球的直径却有着12,000多公里呢！就是说，假定地球像一个大皮球那么大，那末，我们的眼睛所能直接和间接看到的一层就只有一张纸那么厚。再深些的地方究竟是什么样子，我们有没有什么办法去侦察呢？有。这就是靠由地震的各种震波给我们传送来的消息。不过，通过地震波获得有关地下情况的消息，只能帮助我们了解地下的物质的大概样子，不能像我们在地表所看见的岩石那么清楚。

地球深处的物质，对我们现在生活上的关系较少。和我们关系最密切的，还是石圈的最上一层。我们的老祖宗曾经用石头来制造石斧、石刀、石钻、石箭等等从事劳动的工具。今天我们不再需要石器了，可是，我们现在种地或在工厂里、矿山里劳动所需的工具和日常需要的东西，仍然还要往石圈里要原料。只是跟着人类的进步，向石圈索取这些原料的数量和种类都是越来越多了，并且向石圈探查和开采这些原料的工具和技术，也就越来越进步了。

最近几十年来，从石圈中不断地发现了各种具有新的用途的原料。比如能够分裂并大量发热的放射性矿物，如铀、钍等类，我们已经能够加以利用，例如用来开动机器、促进庄稼生长、治疗难治的疾病等等。将来，人们还要利用原子能来推动各种机器和一切交通运输工具，要它们驯服地

65

《看看我们的地球》正文。

李四光部長接見地質力

1962年1月23日李四光（一排正中）与地质力学讲习班全体学员合影。

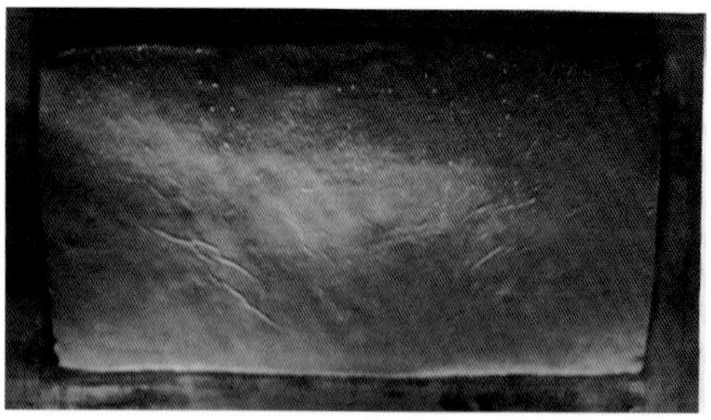

1

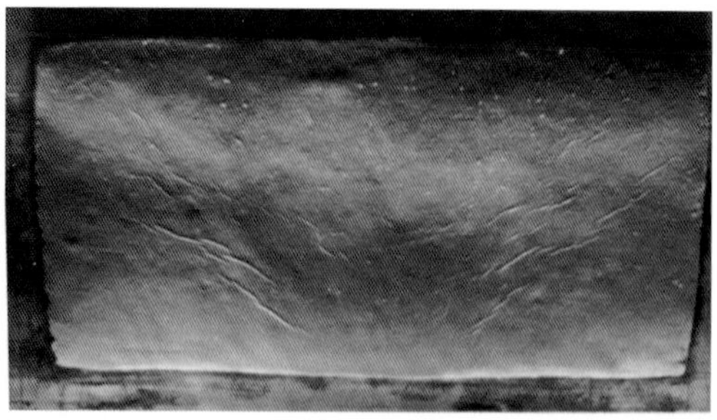

2

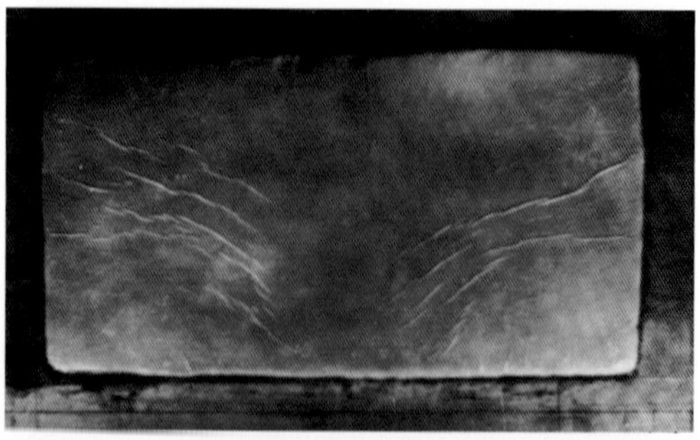

3

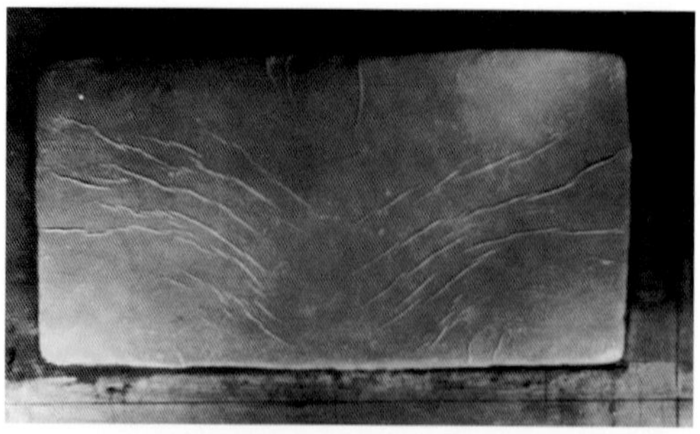

4

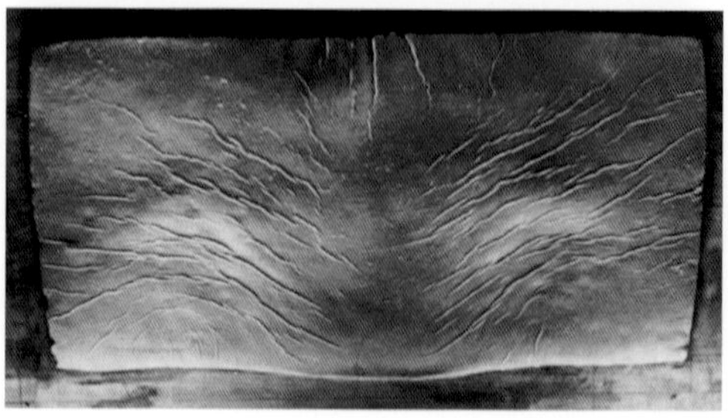

5

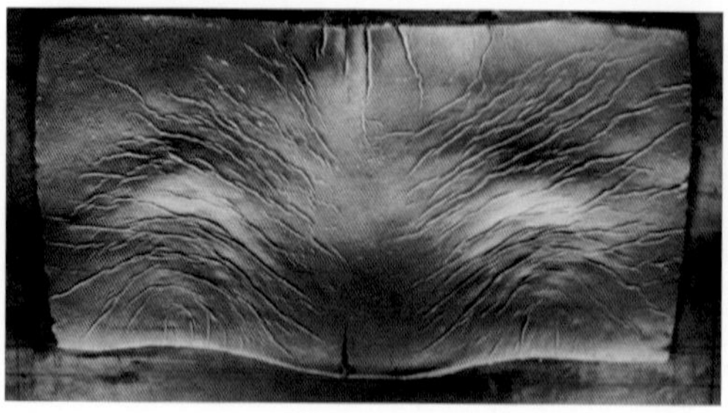

6

模拟试验是李四光研究地质构造运动的手段之一，其中之一是泥巴实验。这一组照片从1至6显示了一个山字型构造的形成过程。图中泥巴模型尺寸为60厘米×30厘米。

在李四光养病期间，对石油工作一直非常关心。他多次同地质部领导同志一起研究如何打开局面的问题。地质部党组根据李四光的意见，认为目前已经找到的油田，多偏居西北地区，按目前交通情况，在短期内大量开发供应全国的需要，还有相当困难。因此，必须在保持西北、西南石油地质普查工作继续前进的同时，把工作重点转向我国工业基础较强、交通又比较便利的东部地区。党中央批准了地质部党组的这个意见，从而确定了第二个五年计划期间石油地质普查工作“不放弃西北，多搞东部”的正确方针。松辽、四川、苏北、华北等地区被列为全国石油普查的重点地区，实现了我国找油工作的“战略东移”，产生了深远的影响。

地质部松辽石油普查大队，经过1956、1957两年的地质、钻探和物探工作，对松辽构造得到了进一步的认识，肯定了松辽盆地是很有希望的含油盆地。这时，石油部的队伍也开进松辽平原。从此两支兄弟队伍，同心协力，并肩战斗在茫茫草原上。1958年2月，石油工业部和地质部共同发出了“三年攻下松辽”的战斗号召。地质部从四川、青海、陕甘宁调集队伍，加强松辽找油工作，同时组成东北石油物探大队，开始进行地震勘探。在吉林省扶余县（今扶余市）前郭旗（今松原市前郭尔罗斯蒙古族自治县）的一个钻井中，首次遇见厚达17厘米和50厘米的油砂岩层。6月，又在公主岭西北杨大城子镇附近的一个钻井中，遇到了一个新的厚度在三米以上的含油砂岩层，岩芯取出后有原油渗出。新华社根据这个资料，发出了《松辽平原有石油》的消息报道，报道中说："松辽平原不久将成为我国重要的油区之一。"

9月，李四光会见松辽石油普查大队负责人，对他们的工作表示十分满意。李四光满面笑容地说："毛主席和党中央其他领导同志，对石油非常关心，把石油比作像吃饭一样重要。"又说："松辽出油，别开生面。""现在出油的地区，是站住了。"李四光详细地听取了他们在松辽地区所取得的地质成果的

1953年李四光和在秦皇岛野外实习的北京地质学院学生一起吃午饭。

汇报之后，又指出："搞石油要把眼光放远一些，要从长远考虑，不能仅限于现存老油区附近。"他指出，松辽大凹陷，不论其成因如何，确是存在的。它被大隆起所环围，西面和东南有北北东方向的大兴安岭和长白山脉，北面是小兴安岭及位于苏联的近东西向褶皱隆起带，南面是近东西向的阴山山脉及其东延部分。如何能找出大凹陷的分布规律，了解其产生的原因，对找石油是非常重要的。实际上大凹陷和隆起的分布是有规律的。李四光向他们介绍了新华夏系三个沉降带的分布情形之后说："这个新华夏系构造带，中间多为近东西向复杂构造带所分隔，而且东西向构造带更向东延入海域，其东端则指向太平洋西岸各岛弧的连结处，这是很有意思的。""我们找油的远景区，就是这些被隆起所划分出来的盆地或平原地区。"李四光还明确指出："在松辽盆地南面的隆起上找油，可能希望很小。更向南沿渤海湾及渤海内，可能是找油的好地方。因此跨过东西向隆起带向南去找油是非常重要的。"李四光的这次谈话，对松辽石油普查大队的同志鼓舞很大，使他们的眼界更加开阔了，干劲也更大了。

国庆十周年即将来临，石油工业部在黑龙江省肇州县高台子构造松基3井，首次获得自喷工业油流；紧接着，地质部在吉林省扶余县雅达红构造扶27井，也获得工业油流。我国东部找油取得了具有历史意义的突破，迎来了1960年大庆油田大会战的胜利。

在这之后，李四光更加强调构造体系对油区的控制，并及时地对全国石油地质工作提出了新的战略部署。1959年10月，松辽石油普查大队向地质部汇报的时候，李四光指出："看来松辽油区大局已定，今后该是我们跳出门坎（指公主岭以南地区地下埋伏的东西隆起带）往南移动的时候了（意指辽河下游、渤海及华北平原）。"12月，地质部召开石油普查专业会议，李四光对当前的石油普查和勘探方向，提出了七个新的重要工作地区：一、海拉尔—巴音和硕区。这个地区以东，越过大兴安岭就是松辽平原。它和鄂尔多斯盆地以及四川盆地在一条线上。对大兴安岭和它向西南延伸的隆起地带来说，它们是属于同一沉降带，只是由于被隔离而成为三个盆地。四川盆地、鄂尔多斯盆地都是含油地区，所以这个盆地本身也大有可能是一个油区。二、在松辽平原北部，已经发现多层油砂，并流出原油。为了迅速开展普查工作，在辽河平原的下游，也应该进行工作。三、在辽河平原的南部和华

1953年在秦皇岛野外实习的北京地质学院学生
赠送给李四光一尊地质工作者的石膏像。

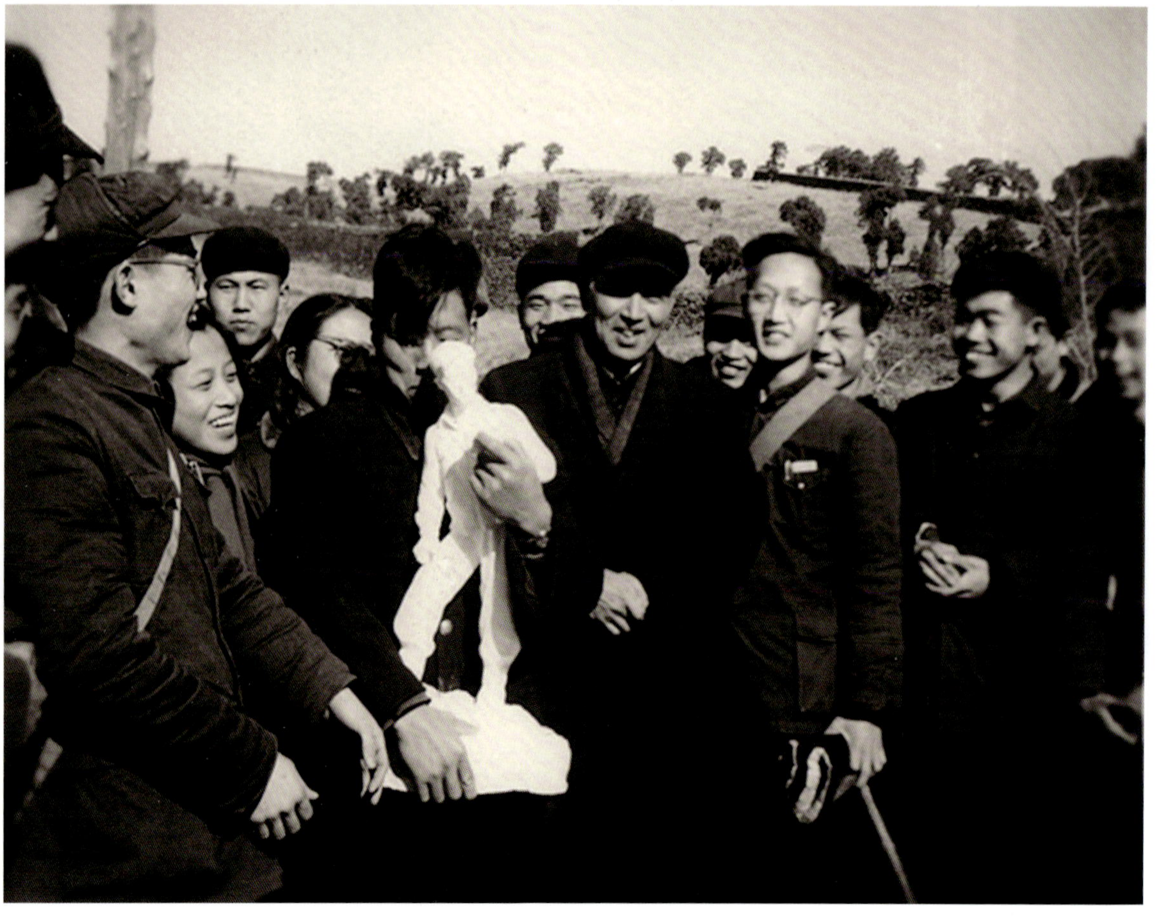

1961年8月李四光（二排右三）乘中国科学院海洋研究所海洋调查船“金星号”到海阳县（今海阳市）、乳山县（今乳山市）海域考察后和全体研究人员及船员合影。

北平原的北部，经过普查，如果发现有油气苗显示，就应该在渤海方面进行普查乃至钻探工作。四、其他若干离海岸不远的海洋区域，也值得开展普查乃至进行钻探。五、关于在鄂尔多斯盆地寻找具有工业价值油田的工作，根据四川盆地的经验，也应该对中部地区的构造，加强普查和勘探。六、柴达木盆地、西藏地区若干较大的山间盆地，应该作为石油普查、勘探的对象。在那里，丁青和黑河以西某些地点，曾经发现了沥青和油砂。西藏东南部，包括波密地区，与印度的阿萨姆油田相距不远，它储油的可能是值得重视的。七、塔里木盆地，位于柴达木盆地和准噶尔盆地之间。既然柴达木和准噶尔已经证实是广大的油区，对塔里木开展普查勘探工作，也是具有意义的。

1962年10月李四光到地质力学研究所食堂看望职工。

1962年李四光和地质力学进修班的学员座谈。

1962年10月26日地质部领导在李四光居所饭厅为李四光庆祝73岁生日。

1961年9月，李四光根据当时已经取得的地质资料，进一步分析我国东部油田的分布规律，给地质部党组写了一封信。信中说："最近石油勘探工作的进展，令人感到振奋。华北和华中若干钻探地点多层油砂的发现，很清楚，不仅标志着其中某些地区是具有工业价值的油田，而且在更广泛的意义上，甚至可以说，在更重大的意义上，再一次证明了把华北平原、江

1962年春李四光在紫竹院新居院内种树。

汉平原和松辽平原联系起来作为新华夏系沉降带中三个段落的看法是正确的。”“所谓江汉平原，实际上应该包括全部华中平原和两湖盆地，它还可能在越过南岭以后，继续沿着南南西的方向伸展到广东的西南部乃至北部湾。”信中还说：“不过肯定一个油区的范围是一回事，圈定一个油田另是一回事。一个油区的构造有它自己的特点，在同一油区中各个油田的构造也有它们的共同点。如果新华夏系沉降带是由于新华夏系构造运动而形成的第一级构造，那么，其中各个油田，就应该受到跟着这个第一级构造而产生的第二级、第三级甚至更低级再次构造的控制。”

10月，地质部党组经过讨论，同意李四光的意见，并及时向周恩来总理做了报告。地质部党组在报告中说，“党组同意李四光同志的理论”，“地质部几年来的石油地质工作，就是按照李四光同志的意见布置进行的”。事实证明，“李四光同志的理论是符合中国油田分布规律的客观实际的”。报告还说：“新华夏构造体系的沉降带占有很大的面积。几年以来，我们已进

1962年春李四光在紫竹院新居院内搞绿化。他用的推车是他自己设计的，前面的挡板可以从上面拉出来，方便装卸土。

1962年春李四光在紫竹院新居。

1962年冬李四光夫妇在居所院内和地质力学研究所人员合影。

1962年10月李四光夫妇和地质部、地质力学研究所的同事在紫竹院住所大门前合影。

1962年10月李四光夫妇和秘书、警卫在紫竹院新居大门前合影。

1962年10月李四光夫妇及他的秘书在新居大门前和地质力学研究所领导合影。立者左起：杨开庆、吴磊伯、陈庆宣、李四光、徐恩溥、许淑彬、孙殿卿，前排蹲者左起：马胜云、陈群。

1962年春李四光在紫竹院居所中的
办公室向匈牙利地质科学家赠书。

1962年春李四光在紫竹院居所大门前和来访的匈牙利地质科学家合影。一排右三是何长工，二排右一是肖赤。

行了不少工作，但还有许多地区须继续工作。”“在目前，为了贯彻调整、巩固、充实、提高以及缩短战线、保证重点的方针，党组意见，今后一二年内仍须以华北为重点，然后逐步南移，有计划有步骤地开展各个地区的工作。”

1962年初，李四光迁到北京西郊紫竹院居住。

9月，石油工业部在山东广饶东营的深钻，突破了富集油层，高产原油连续喷出达数月之久，创造了当时国内产量最高的油井。这就是现在的胜利油田。同时，地质部在沾化义和庄、黄骅羊三木，也发现了不稳定的油流和相当厚的多层油砂。这就是现在的大港油田。把华北平原作为一个油区的预想，经过勘探实践，继松辽之后，也得到了证实。

通过松辽、华北及其他地区的石油普查勘探工作所取得的经验，李四光对油区及油田的一般勘探程序，特别是对那些表面被新地层覆盖，岩层露头很少，缺乏油气显示的地区，提出了具体的工作步骤。

1962年春李四光在紫竹院居所中的办公室向匈牙利地质科学家赠书。

1963年春李四光在居所办公室会见朝鲜地质代表团。

1963年春李四光在居所办公室向朝鲜地质代表团介绍构造体系概念。

1963年春李四光在居所大门外和朝鲜地质代表团合影。

1963年春李四光在居所会见朝鲜地质代表团，
和何长工一起送代表团离开。

1963年一个夏夜李四光夫妇在居所院内假山旁。

1964年初夏李四光在居所会议室会见苏联地质学家。

1964年初夏李四光在紫竹院居所院内送前来拜访的苏联地质学家。

1963年11月，第二届全国人民代表大会举行第四次会议。会上，李富春副总理代表国务院做的报告中正式宣布了松辽油田的成就，并指出这一成就，是在我国自力更生、奋发图强的方针指导下取得的。与会代表非常振奋。我国需要的石油，过去绝大部分依靠进口，现在已经可以基本自给了。

1964年元旦的晚上，毛泽东主席特意请李四光到怀仁堂一起观看现代豫剧《朝阳沟》。李四光当时的心情十分激动。毛主席高兴地对李四光说："你们两家（指地质部和石油工业部）都有很大的功劳！"演出结束后，毛主席又请李四光同中央领导同志一起接见演员，合影留念。

12月，第三届全国人民代表大会召开。李四光出席了大会，听取了周恩来总理的政府工作报告。周总理在报告中指出："第一个五年计划建设起来的大庆油田，是根据我国地质专家独创的石油地质理论进行勘探而发现的。"会议期间的一天，李四光刚走进人民大会堂，一位工作人员对他说："李老，请你到北京厅去一下！"李四光来到北京厅门口，刚跨进一只脚，发现毛主席在里面，他喊了一声："主席。"忙又抬脚向后退去，一边抱歉地对毛主席说："主席，对不起，我走错了门。"这时，毛主席走过来，紧握住李四光的手，亲切地说："没有走错，是我找你。李老，你的太极拳打得不错啊！"一时，李四光不明白毛主席这话的意思，心想，毛主席怎么知道我打太极拳呢？他认真地解释说："前几年动手术，身体不太好，在杭州学过一阵太极拳，但打得不好。"毛主席请李四光在沙发上坐下来，谈的却是石油问题。这时，李四光才恍然大悟，原来毛主席说的打太极拳是指找油。

1964年元旦李四光应毛泽东主席邀请观看豫剧《朝阳沟》，谢幕后与中央领导同志一起会见演员。

毛泽东主席的几次接见和谈话，周恩来总理在全国人民代表大会上的报告中对石油地质理论的肯定，都是对李四光在科学工作方面的高度评价，也是对他极其亲切的鼓励。当然，李四光并不满足已经取得的成绩。他总感到“地质部在发现油田、拿下油田方面应当是开路先锋，应该承担这一方面的任务”。而且，从现在已经探明的石油储量来看，还远远落后于国民经济发展的需要，要做的工作还很多。过去几年的工作，有成功的一面，也有失败的教训，都需要及时总结，使工作前进得更快一些。

1964年12月全国政协四届一次会议上毛泽东主席与李四光握手交谈。

在李四光的科学生活中，同英、美、苏、德、法、挪威、印度、匈牙利、捷克、日本、新西兰等国的地质学家、地理学家和有关的科学家，不断有著作交换和信件往来。只是因为新中国成立前他的生活不安定，这些书信几乎都没有能够保存下来。现在我们看到的，主要是新中国成立后的信件。通过这些交往，李四光及时地了解到现代科学发展的状况，从中吸取必要的养料，也从中得到鼓舞和力量。

英国，是李四光学习地质的地方。在英国地质学界，提起中国学者“J. S. Lee”，不少人都称赞“他确是一位非常了不起的人”。早在1929年，李四光就是伦敦地质学会的国外会员。1960年初，英国皇家学会会员李约瑟博士的巨著《中国科学技术史》第三卷问世。这是李约瑟献给李四光和竺可桢两人的。李四光和竺可桢对于李约瑟这种深情的表示，感到很惭愧，因为他们基本上没有给这部巨著的编写工作提供什么帮助。2月，他们联名给李约瑟写信表达了这种不安的心情，并说：“这本书将在广阔范围内使人们了解到古代的中国人民如何地打开大自然的秘密和克服他们在日常生活中所遇到的困难付出了劳动，同时也增进人们对中国科学技术发展过程的了解和东西方人民间的友谊。因此，您把这本书的第三卷献给我们俩人，使我们感到莫大的荣幸。”

1959年李约瑟在他的《中国科学技术史》一书的扉页上题写：将此书献给竺可桢、李四光。

李四光同著名的印度古植物学家萨尼，是早年在英国相识的。经萨尼推荐，李四光一直是印度古生物学会会员。这个学会，每年要召开一次年会，都通知李四光参加。李四光因工作繁忙不能出席时，也总是打电报或写信，向年会表示祝贺。李四光在印度地质界是受到尊敬的。1956年7月，瓦底纳博士通过中国驻印大使馆，给李四光送来了一本他的新作《印度地质学》，并且写了一封热情洋溢的信，渴望李四光能到印度去访问。李四光对瓦底纳的情谊十分感激，他在回信中说："多少年过去了，我一直在寻找您的内容丰富的著作，以期学习你们伟大国家的地质情况。现在这个愿望实现了。您的这部著作，把我们之间的友谊紧紧地连在一起。"李四光还说："随着我们两国人民交往日益增进，我相信，不久的将来，我们能够有机会，在一起讨论我们共同关心的问题。"

李四光同苏联地质、地理学家们的联系和友谊，并不是新中国成立后才开始的。早在1925年9月，李四光荣幸地到列宁格勒和莫斯科参加苏联科学院成立200周年纪念大会，会见了不少苏联的科学家。李四光还一直是全苏古生物学会的荣誉会员。新中国成立后，李四光与苏联同行学者的联系比过去更密切了。特别是20世纪50年代，李四光的《中国地质学》《旋卷构造及其他有关中国西北部大地构造体系复合问题》两部著作被译成俄文在苏联发行之后，他经常收到苏联同行学者寄来的书信，共同探讨学术上的问题。苏联科学家们对李四光在发展地质科学方面的贡献给予很高的评价。1958年6月，苏联科学院全体大会一致选举李四光为苏联科学院院士。1959年12月，苏联科学院主席团决定授予李四光卡尔宾斯基金质奖章。克鲁包特金教授在《自然》杂志上撰文，介绍了李四光在地质科学上的成就。

1964年夏李四光夫妇和地质力学研究所的同事在北京郊区郊游。

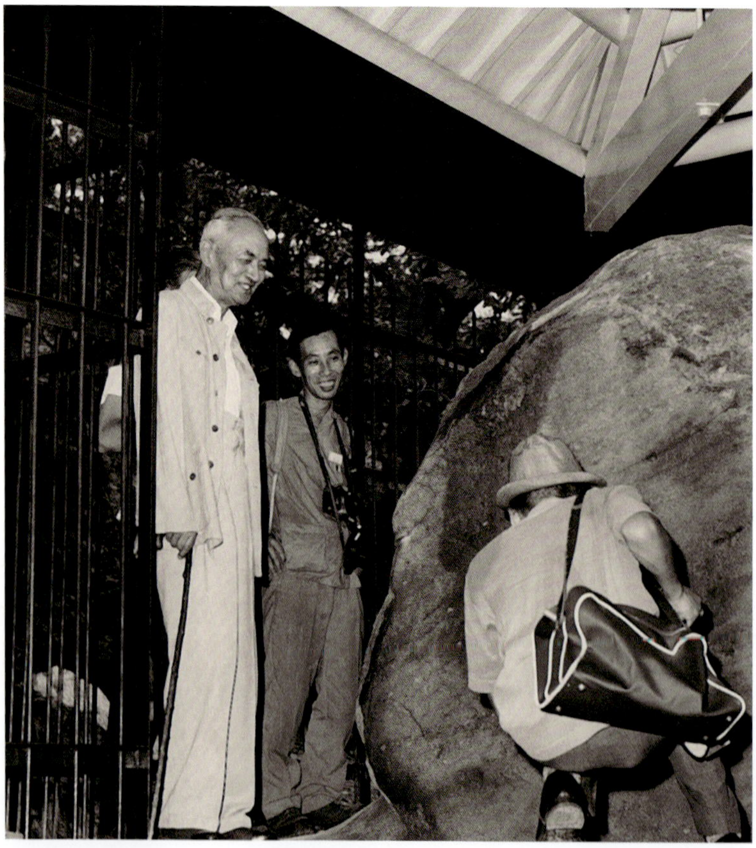

1964年7月李四光到北京西山八大处考察北京文化局为八大处六处下桥边带有冰溜擦痕的巨型漂砾所建的亭子，并题字“冰川漂砾”。

1964年7月李四光在冰川考察途中休息并开现场讨论会。

1964年8月，国际科学讨论会在北京举行。参加这次讨论会的，有亚洲、非洲、拉丁美洲和大洋洲44个国家和地区的367位科学家。讨论会开幕前夕，陈毅副总理在招待会上致辞。会议期间，毛泽东、刘少奇、朱德等党和国家领导人分别接见了参加讨论会的全体科学家。李四光特意在西山八大处会见各国地质学家和古生物学家，并且进行了一次有趣的短程地质旅行。李四光同各国科学家一起登上西山的高处，观看第四纪冰川遗迹，然后来到山腰一处古松覆盖的平台上。这里摆着桌子和藤椅，桌子上陈列着李四光多年收集的冰川沉积物和岩石力学方面的标本，以及华北地区第四纪时海侵的资料。李四光亲自一一介绍给各国同行。北京科学讨论会闭幕时，四大洲的科学家们同首都各界人士1万人欢聚在人民大会堂。有39个国家和地区科学团体的科学家，先后登台讲话。闭幕大会从上午9时开始，到下午6时结束。李四光在闭幕会上致辞。他说："1964年北京科学讨论会是四大洲科学家第一次互相观摩大会。在会议上宣读和讨论的200多篇科学论文，从不同的角度展示了四大洲各国科学事业的蓬勃发展。这是一次绚丽多彩、成果丰硕的科学讨论会。"他还说："各国同行们在参观访问之后，将先后返回自己的祖国，从事科学工作。我们各大洲之间相距虽然很远，我们的心情却是很接近的。中国有一句古诗：'海内存知己，天涯若比邻。'共同斗争中产生的友谊把我们紧密地连结在一起。"

1964年8月北京国际科学讨论会上李四光会见参加会议的各国科学家。

1964年8月北京国际科学讨论会上李四光和非洲科学家握手。

1964年8月北京国际科学讨论会上李四光和非洲科学家亲切交谈。

1964年8月北京国际科学讨论会上
李四光和科学家做学术交流。

1964年8月北京国际科学讨论会上李四光向
科学家们介绍中国构造地质的研究状况。

1964年8月李四光陪同参加北京科学讨论会的各国科学家到西山八大处参观冰川漂砾。

1964年8月北京国际科学讨论会上李四光向国外地质学家、古生物学家介绍冰川沉积物和岩石力学方面的标本。

1964年8月北京国际科学讨论会上李四光向国外地质学家、古生物学家介绍冰川沉积物和岩石力学方面的标本、资料。前排右一：李四光。后排左起：马杏垣、黄汲清、程裕淇、张文佑。

1964年8月28日，李四光和地质力学研究所的科研人员在香山讨论工作。

1964年冬李四光在北京西山卧佛寺后面樱桃沟内小憩。

1965年春节李四光夫妇在居所办公室外走廊上。

鞠躬尽瘁
Persisting to the End
(1965—1971)

1965年2月，李四光在北京医院门诊检查身体时，发现左下腹有一搏动性肿块，随后经北京医院约请张孝骞、吴蔚然等内外科专家会诊，确诊为左髂骨总动脉瘤。7月，北京医院向国务院写了一份关于李四光病情的报告，考虑到病人已76岁高龄，又患有冠状动脉硬化性心脏病，并且已将左肾切除，因此专家们认为手术复杂，危险性很大，宜密切观察，同时又要做好手术准备。从这以后，国务院决定，非特别需要并经过周恩来总理同意的，李四光

1965年春李四光和夫人许淑彬在紫竹院家中庭院里。

可以不参加任何活动。周总理在百忙中还特意请邓颖超几次来探望过李四光。经过一段时间的观察，医生们发现，只要适当地限制工作时间，加强室外轻微活动，同时用药物控制血压，效果还是比较好的。

自从发现动脉瘤之后，李四光总感到说不定什么时候自己可能会突然躺倒的，时间是不多了，但还有许多工作要做：地质力学的总结工作，才写完第一篇《地质力学概论》，地震预报的探索刚刚起步，地热资源的开发与利用还没有得到广泛的重视……想到这些，李四光的心情十分不安。他思索着如何加快步伐，抓紧进行这些未了的工作。

1965年3月，第一届全国构造地质学术会议在北京开幕。李四光出席了这次会议，并在会上就构造地质学方面的几个重要的争论问题，做了启发性的发言。他请大家认真读一读毛泽东主席的《实践论》和《人的正确思想是从哪里来的》两篇著作，他认为只要有了这样的思想做指导，再来摆事实、讲道理，那么问题总有一天会得到解决的。会议结束时，他还为大会做了总结发言，明确地提出了要改进构造地质工作的问题。他说，通过这次会议，大家对构造地质工作如何紧密地和生产实践结合起来，都有了比较明确的认识。因为不管你对地质构造现象有什么样的看法，构造地质工作的目的，总应该是为生产服务的。正确的理论是实践的总结，实践又是理论的验证。不

1965年初冬李四光和地质部领导在居所大门前合影。前排左起：许杰、胥光义、李四光、许淑彬。前排右二：宋应。

待言，那些空讲大道理，不能用来解决实际问题的理论是没有用处的，也是不成其为理论的。理论联系实际，既包括当前迫切需要解决的问题，又包括为了长期打算而从事探索性的问题。脱离实际去搞理论固然不对，根本不要理论去指导实际工作也是不对的。

为了使地质力学的研究工作今后能够继续下去，并有所发展，6月29日，李四光特地修订了《地质力学的方法与实践》的提纲。他坚信，只要沿着提纲的路子走下去，地质力学就有可能日臻完善。他还同地质力学进修班的学员谈地质力学的发展过程和当前的任务，并回答他们提出的问题。

我国是一个多震的国家，地震现象较为普遍。大力开展地震地质和地震预报工作，是一项刻不容缓的重大任务。李四光一直很重视这项工作。旧中国的地震科学工作，比起地质工作来，更不受重视，因此基础更为薄弱。1950年初，原南京中央地质调查所不到十个人的地震研究室和原中央研究院有关研究所合并，成立中国科学院地球物理研究所。地震工作任务首先落到了中国科学院。1953年中国科学院成立地震工作委员会，李四光兼任主任委员。委员会下设综合、地质、历史等几个小组。李四光曾几次找范文澜商谈如何收集分析中国历史文献中丰富的地震记载，以弥补科学记录不足的问题。1952年10月山西崞县地区和1954年2月甘肃山丹地区先后发生地震，李四光都亲自指派地质人员参加实地调查，亲自听取调查汇报，多次参加讨论地震强度和烈度划分的会议。他还在《旋卷构造及其他有关中国西北部大地构造体系复合问题》一书

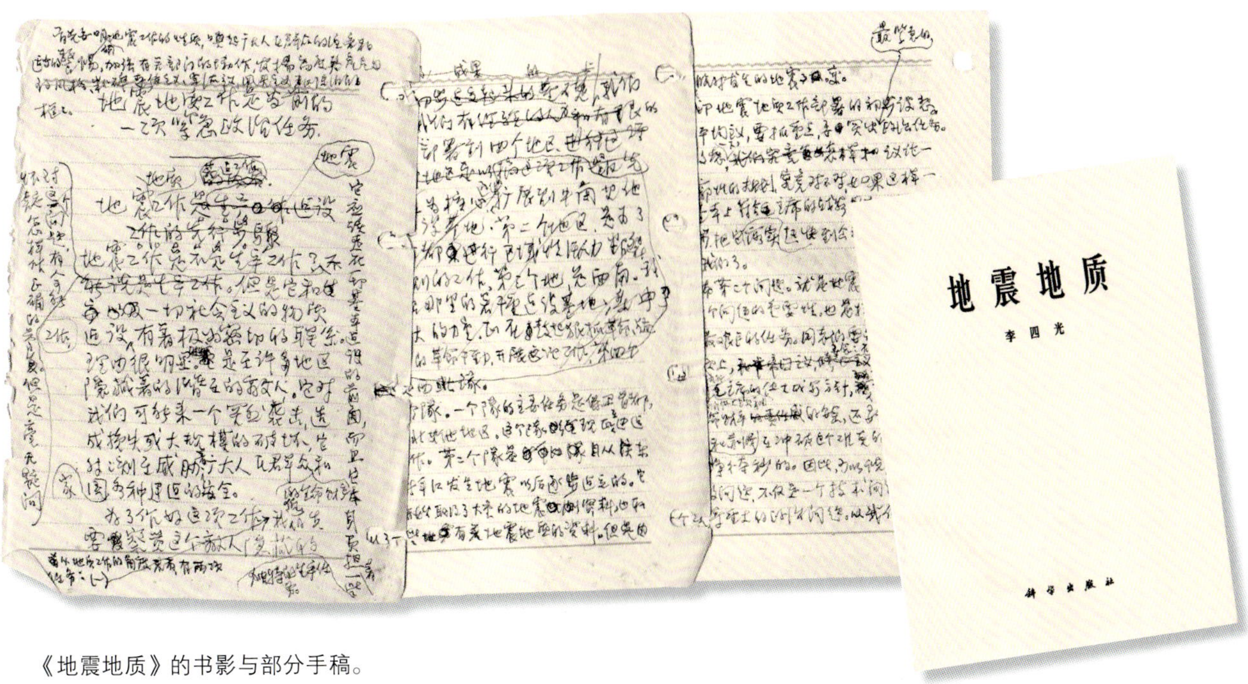

《地震地质》的书影与部分手稿。

中，专门论述了中国西北部活动性构造体系与地震带分布的关系。1955年中国科学院地震工作委员会改由竺可桢副院长主持，此后李四光仍经常关心着这项工作。1962年广东新丰江水库发生地震，特别是1966年河北邢台地区发生强烈地震以后，更使李四光感到焦虑，在他生命的最后几年里，他用了很大的精力来抓地震预报的工作，可以说这是他逝世前最放心不下的一件大事。

在我国，许多地震的产生，是由地质构造运动引起的。这种现象，简单地说，就是由于地下岩层发生比较剧烈的破坏性变动，它所产生的能量，通过岩层的波动，向上下四周传播，直至达到地表各点。因此，应该从地质构造的角度来研究地震问题，把构造地质工作和地震工作密切地结合起来。这就是我们所说的地震地质工作。

李四光认为，地震地质工作的主要任务，应该是：侦察地震这个地下“敌人”的潜伏场所，并监视它的活动，为保卫广大人民生命财产和社会主义建设的安全服务。它的内容可以包括下列三项程序：首先，要对有关地区详尽地进行地质构造调查工作，特别要查明出露地表的具有活动性的断裂带的性质、分布规律和延伸范围；同时，要尽量收集历史地震资料，加以综合分析，并根据这些资料，研究构造体系和地震的关系。这样，就可以发现潜在危险地区。第二，围绕现今还在活动的断裂带，进行精密大地测量和微量位移测量，并设置地震观测网，进行微观的和宏观的地震观测工作。第三，加强构造应力场的研究，观测和分析现今地应力分布的情况、活动的方式和

1970年李四光为研究北京周边地震地质条件在延庆县（今延庆区）山区考察地质构造，观察岩层走向。

1970年李四光为研究北京周边地震地质条件在延庆县山区考察地质构造。

1 | 2
3 | 4

1、2—1970年夏李四光在河北三河地震地质大队做报告，讲述他对地震地质工作和地震预报的设想及实施。

3、4—1970年夏李四光到地震观测台和地应力观测站听取工作汇报。

变化的规律，从而明确它们和当地地震的关系，并确定震源的所在和分布的范围。此外，对于受力作用的岩石的各种性质，也应认真研究。经过对上述资料的综合分析，我们就有可能推测地震发生的趋势。

1966年3月8日，河北邢台地区发生七级以上的强烈地震，震区位于隆尧、宁晋、新河、巨鹿四县接壤地带。由于地震引起地表广泛变形，地面大幅度升降，大量裂隙密集成带出现，沿裂隙带普遍发生涌泉冒砂，霎时墙倒屋坍，道路、桥梁、堤坝以及农田建设均遭到了严重破坏，人民生命财产遭到巨大损失。

当天下午，李四光出席了周恩来总理召开的救灾工作会议。根据会议精神，李四光亲自组织了一个地震地质考察小队，连夜派往震区。3月22日，邢台地区又发生了一次强烈地震。为了研究邢台地震发展的趋势，周总理几次召开会议进行讨论，李四光都出席了。周总理请李四光发表意见。李四光把随身带来的尧山地应力变化曲线图摊开，向周总理一一做了介绍。为了把情况弄得更准确一些，他还立即在会场给尧山地应力观测站打电话，问清了当时现场的电感值有无变化；然后，他回答周总理提出的问题说，根据现有资料，邢台地区已经发生了两次强震和万余次较小的地震，基岩至少是上层破坏得很厉害，产生了大量的裂隙，即使再有地应力积累情况的重演，那些积累起来的应力，大

测量元件摆放的岩芯。

测量地应力的元件。

邢台地震发生后，李四光加速了对地应力的测量和研究。他亲自设计测量地应力的元件，经实验证明地震对地应力变化的影响。

部分都可能通过裂隙的活动释放能量，所以在邢台地区及其邻近属于同一构造体系的地区，再发生像3月8日和3月22日那样强烈地震的可能性不大。当然，在华北平原还未平静之前，一系列较小的地震可能还会继续一个时期。但是，就整个华北平原来看，“震源带有可能向东北方向发展的趋势”。4月10日，在周总理召集的研究地震发展趋势的会上，李四光还明确提出：“从构造体系上看，深县（今深州市）、沧州（今沧州市）、河间（今河间市）这些地区发生地震的可能性是不能忽视的。”这个问题，直接关系到京津地区的安全。一年之后，即1967年3月，河间地区发生了六点三级地震，证实了李四光的这一推测。

在紧张的工作中，李四光受到周总理两次亲临灾区视察的强烈感召，也很想到邢台去看一看。但是，由于动脉瘤等疾病，医生嘱咐他不能有过多或过重的体力活动；在家里，夫人也反对。后来，经过李四光的耐心说服，夫人终于同意了他的邢台之行。4月22日，李四光乘火车赴尧山考察。经过这次实地考察，李四光亲自指导了邢台地震地质考察队编写《邢台地震地质初步考察报告》的工作。报告根据地震区地表大量形变的实际资料，论证了地表形变与基岩构造特征之间的关系，分析了地震发生的原因和可能扩展的趋势，提出了解决地震预报的新途径。

多年来，世界上不少国家都在研究地震预报，但都没有得到令人满意的结果。我国也是如此。地震能不能预报？李四光坚信，地震是可以预报的。世界上没有解决的问题，为什么我们就不能解决？5月28日，周恩来总理在接见邢台地震科学讨论会代表时的讲话中，称赞李四光这种“独排众议”的勇于探索的精神。但是，作为地质部和中国科学院的主要领导人之一，李四光觉得这项工作抓得晚了一点。为此，他感到十分内疚，他决心利用这次邢台地震的机会，把地震预报工作推进一大步。他和年轻的地震地质工作者一起，在这方面做了许多有意义的工作。这些工作，除了上面已经提到的以外，还有这样两个例子：1967年10月，李四光在国家科委地震办公室研究地下水观测的会上指出：“应向滦县、迁安地区做些观测。如果这些地区活动的话，那就很难排除大地震的发生。”九年以后，1976年7月28日，唐山发生了7.8级地震，当晚滦县又出现了7.1级强余震。

1968年2月，李四光在听了国家科委地震办公室汇报京津地区的地震情况之后说：“我看，北京地区处于比较安全的地位。对北京的情况我还是比较乐观的。”就是这次谈话后不久，在一个深夜里，他接到国务院召开紧急会议的通知。当他赶到会议厅时已近凌晨两点钟。周总理请李四光在他的身边坐下。这时，正在研究有关方面向国务院的报告，说当天清晨七时北京将要发生7级地震，请国务院批准立即通知北京居民搬到室外去居住。会上各种意见都讲过了。周总理问李四光，情况如何，真是这样紧急吗？李四光先问了一下情况，了解到他们主要是根据北京附近的小震突然平静，一些动物表现很不安宁，因此提出可能发生7级地震。这时，李四光还是采取过去的办法，给北京附近的一些地应力观测站打电话了解情况，都反映说没有发现什么异常。李四光这才对周总理说：“根据邢台等地区地应力的长期观测，有大震，一般都是有变化的。……看来，今晚不一定要发警报，当然要密切注意观察。”周总理同意不发警报，并说：“李老你年纪大了，身体不好，早点回去休息吧！”这时，已是凌晨三点左右了。但是，这一夜，周总理并没有休息，为了首都人民的安全，一直在国务院办公室监视新情况的发生，一直等到平静的黎明来临，冉冉的红日升起。

计算地应力值的草稿。

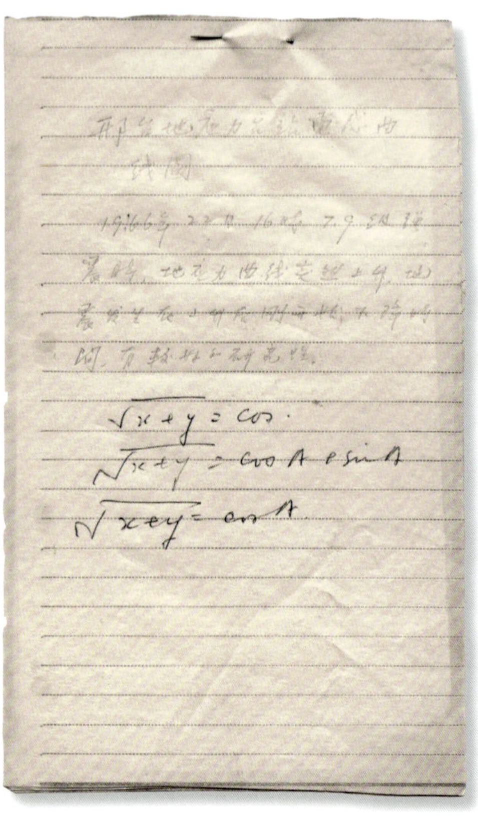

1969年7月18日，渤海发生地震以后，周总理在国务院会议厅召集了有中国科学院、地质部等有关部门负责人参加的会议。会上，周总理就地震工作体制和统一领导问题讲了话。他还宣布，为了加强对地震工作的统一领导，中央决定成立地震工作领导小组，由李四光担任组长。李四光感到自己的担子更重了，为了指导全国的地震工作，保卫京津地区的安全，他经常分析研究大量的观察资料，还多次跋山涉水，深入房山、延庆、密云、三河等地区，调查地震地质现象，视察地震地质工作。这时，他虽已80高龄，而且动脉瘤随时都有破裂的危险，但他不顾个人的安危，

1969年李四光与毛泽东主席交谈，交谈中他告诉毛主席他的左耳听力比较好一些，所以特意将头偏向右面。

把全部心血放在社会主义建设和亿万人民生命财产的安全上。直到他逝世的前一天，他还恳切地对医生说："只要再给我半年的时间，地震预报的探索工作，就会看到结果的。"他对攻破"地震预报"这一难关，始终是满怀信心的。然而，病魔夺去了他的生命，未竟的事业给他留下了深深的遗憾。

1969年5月19日，李四光被毛主席找去谈话。他们从天体起源谈到生命起源。临别时，毛主席说，他很想看李四光写的书，能否送几本给他。同时，还请李四光帮他收集一些国内外的科学资料。并说他不懂英文，最好是编写成中文的。李四光问毛主席想看哪些方面的科学资料。毛主席用手划了个大圈说，就是你研究范围里的资料。李四光很受感动，认为这是毛主席对科学事业的关心。然后，他便立即着手收集有关的科学资料。李四光想，毛主席哪有那么多的时间来看这些东西？不如针对自然科学特别是地质学中的一些重大问题，整理成提纲性的短篇资料。这种资料，力求从前人积累的科学知识中，摄取精华，系统而又简练地把它表达出来。他初步考虑，围绕以下七个方面来编写：一、从地球看宇宙；二、启蒙时代的地质论战；三、总结地层工作的要点；四、古生物及古人类；五、三大冰期；六、地壳的概念；七、地壳构造与地壳运动。就这样，在不到一年的时间里，七篇科学资料整理出来了。总名定为《天文 地质 古生物资料摘要（初稿）》。全书约15万字，并附有60多幅照片和插图。用大字版排印，送给了毛主席和周总理，以及中央其他领导同志和有关部门的负责人。

李四光为毛泽东主席及其他中央领导编写的科学普及书籍《天文 地质 古生物资料摘要（初稿）》。

李四光就收集天文、地质、古生物资料给毛主席的信。

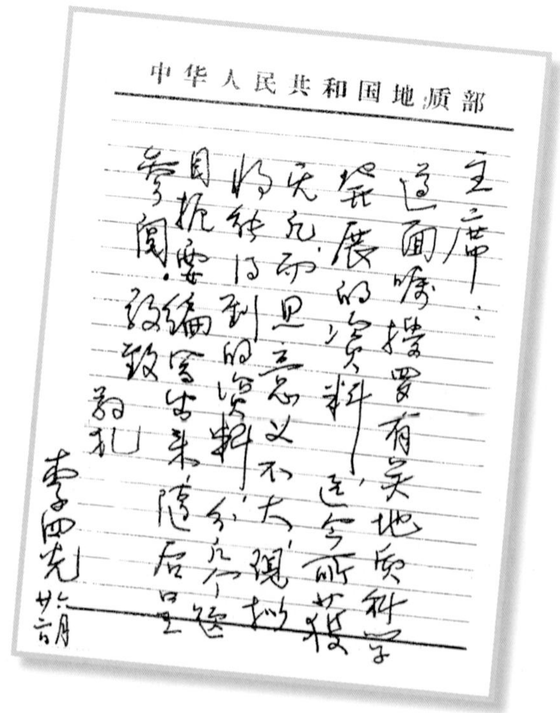
中华人民共和国地质部

主席：

……

致敬礼

李四光

地下热能的开发与利用，同地震预报一样，也是李四光晚年常常挂在心上的一件大事。这件事，在他看来，就像人类发现煤炭、石油可以燃烧一样重要。地热是可供人类利用的一种新能源，也是地质工作的一个新领域。科学的发展告诉人们，煤不仅可以燃烧，而且是很重要的化学工业原料，应该通过各种途径，充分利用煤的各种组成成分，变一用为多用。李四光对世界上蕴藏量有限的煤只被当作燃料烧掉，是十分不安的。早在1956年，他在世界科协成立十周年纪念大会上，曾大声疾呼："用不着想入非非就可以预料到，将来我们的子孙会责怪我们的科学家，为什么眼看着像煤这样贵重的物质被随便当作燃料烧掉而默不作声。"

为了推动地热开发工作，从1958年开始，按照李四光的意见，在地质力学研究室开展了地热学的研究。李四光还亲自推荐年轻的科学工作者到苏联去学习地热学，并且同苏联的地热学家克拉斯科夫斯基教授和留比莫娃教授建立了联系，希望他们提供研究工作的经验。李四光在给留比莫娃的一封信中十分坦率地提出了在中国开展地热学研究尚需解决的四个问题：一是准备在地质力学研究室附近打几个钻孔，其目的在测量地温在长期中可能发生的变化，但是为了保证我们在深井中测定的温度是正确的，不受一切人为的（如钻眼的套管）和自然的（如地下水的浸透）原因的干扰，我们还没有适当的办法；二是我们想利用在全国广泛进行矿产钻探的钻孔来测定地下温度和地温的梯度，为了保证测得的结果正确，就需要掌握一些特殊的技术和使用精密仪器，在这一方面我们毫无经验；三是我们打算逐步展开全国各地区或各项不同的岩石所含微量的和微弱的（包括钾）放射性元素发热量的测定，我们还没有掌握必要的技术来进行这个工作；四是对于核热能的利用，我们感到很大的兴趣，但如何才能鉴定一个足够建立水电站的热液区的存在，在目前我们毫无所知。这反映了李四光对发展我国地热事业的一片苦心。

1970年9月，李四光在武汉听说沙市南面打油井的时候，突然从3000米深处喷出来一股热水，温度达到摄氏100多度，喷了好几天才停下来，把周围的水稻、池塘里的鱼都烫死了。经过化验，原来是一种高温高压的卤水。李四光听了非常高兴。回到北京之后，他要地质力学研究所地热组马上派人去沙市考察。他说，热卤水的价值很高，很宝贵，一定要综合开发，综合利用。不久，李四光又听说天津打出地下热水，并在综合利用方面取得了很好的经验。他高兴极了，不顾别人劝告，决定亲自到天津去考察。李四光这时已81岁高龄，是什么力量促使他这样做呢？回到北京后，他曾对他的女儿这样说："要是把地热充分利用起来，我们可以节省多少燃料！可以给人民的生活造很大的福利……天津、沙市方面已经做出了不少成果，但还只不过是开端，是星星之火。"过了半年多，李四光逝世以后，人们在他经常使用的一个笔记本里发现了一张夹着的纸条，上面写着："在我们这样一个伟大的社会主义国家里，我们中国人民有志气，有力量，克服一切科学技术上的困难，去打开这个无比庞大的热库，让它为人民所利用。""把地球交给我们珍贵的遗产——煤炭之类内容极其丰富的财富，不管青红皂白，一概当作燃

1970年夏李四光到地震观测台和地应力观测站查看数据记录。

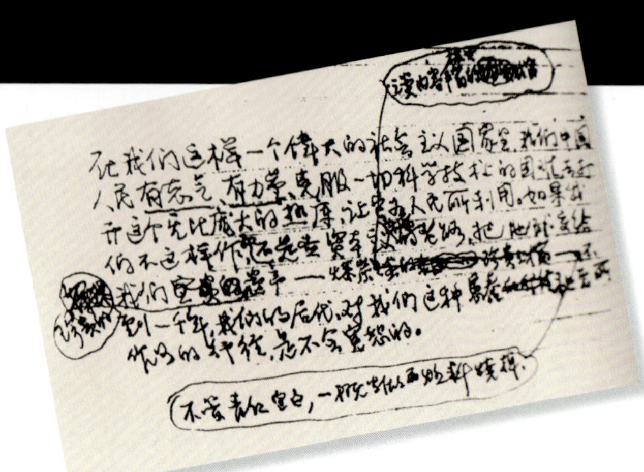

李四光去世后人们在他枕头下面的笔记本里发现的一张纸条，是他就开发地热意见构思的一部分。

1966年春李四光到北京地质学院做学术讲演。

料烧掉，不到一千年，我们的后代，对我们这种愚蠢和无所作为的行径，是不会宽恕的。”

自1965年动脉瘤确诊之后到1971年这六年间，李四光知道自己的生命不长了，但他总是想到自己的一生所做的事情太少了，与党和人民给予他的荣誉相差太远，总希望在剩下的不多的时间里，再努一把力，为科学事业的发展和伟大祖国的繁荣昌盛，多贡献一点力量。在他生命的最后几年，受当时社会环境的影响，他本人和科研工作都受到一些冲击和干扰。在当时十分困

1970年春李四光夫妇为纪念结婚47周年
到紫竹院照相馆照的结婚纪念照。

难的条件下，李四光坚守领导工作和科研工作岗位，经常找有关业务部门和基层单位的工作人员谈话，商量工作，探讨问题。1968年11月，周恩来总理召集中央国家机关各部委军代表和群众代表开会时说："李四光同志是一面旗帜，是辛亥革命的老同志，入党晚了一些，政治上不是动动摇摇的，对社会主义建设做出了很大的贡献，你们要学习他。"1969年4月，在中国共产党第九次全国代表大会上，李四光被选为第九届中央委员会委员。1970年8月，地质部合并到国家计委，成立国家计委地质局后，李四光调任国务院科教组组长。

1971年4月24日，李四光的体温突然上升到38摄氏度，住进了北京医院。28日下午，北京医院约请专家会诊。李四光对医生说："请你们坦率地告诉我，究竟我还有多少时间，让我好安排一下工作……"他还叮嘱身边的工作人员，第二天清早一定要把全国地图集带到医院来。

可是，到29日上午8时30分，由于动脉瘤突然破裂，李四光感到肚子剧烈的疼痛。接着，就休克了。周恩来总理立即派来医务人员，决定施行最后的手术抢救。但是，由于血管硬化，人造血管无法接上，只好进行包扎。当包扎结束时，他的心脏停止了跳动。经过两个多小时的抢救，11时，这位卓越的科学家与世长辞了。享年82岁。

1970年秋李四光夫妇和外孙女在香山卧佛寺樱桃沟花园。

1966年初夏李四光夫妇和女儿在香山卧佛寺大门外。

5月2日下午，是个阴雨天，中共中央、全国人大常委会、全国政协、国务院和中国科学院在八宝山公墓举行告别仪式，沉痛悼念李四光的逝世。告别仪式由郭沫若院长主持，周恩来总理致悼词。周总理告诉大家，刚才收到李四光的女儿李林给他的一封信，他和一些同志商量，就用这封信作为悼词，大家都表示同意。接着，周总理以十分沉痛的心情宣读了这封信。信里主要记述了李四光临终前一天的遗言，以及近几年他经常思考的地震预报、地热利用和海洋地质等方面的问题。李四光那种鞠躬尽瘁、死而后已的精神，催人泪下。

告别仪式结束之后，周总理嘱咐李四光身边的工作人员，一定要把李四光的遗著整理出来。随后来到参加告别仪式的人群之中，周总理沉痛地问大家："刚才念的这封信，你们都听见了吗？""你们一定要继承李四光同志的工作！"

2024年是李四光诞辰135周年。他离开我们已经53年了！但是他的精神永存！他永远是我国科学界的一面旗帜，他的贡献永载科学史册。

1969年冬最后一张全家福。

永远的怀念
Eternal Memory

李四光虽然离开了我们，但他的精神永垂不朽。党和国家领导人、科技界以及各地群众每年都以各种方式纪念李四光，缅怀他的不朽业绩，学习他热爱祖国、无私奉献的精神，以激励自己为社会主义建设事业努力奋斗。

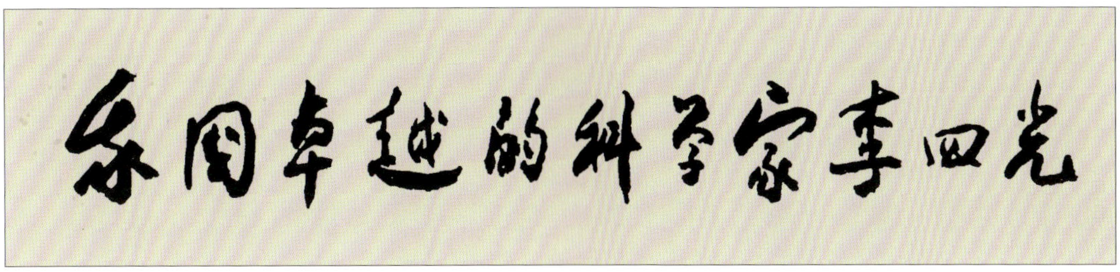

1977年，在李四光去世6年后，郭沫若以81岁高龄欣然为《李四光》连环画题字。

1989年10月26日，中国人民政治协商会议全国委员会、中国科学技术协会、中国科学院和地质矿产部在北京举行了隆重的纪念大会，纪念李四光诞辰100周年。国家主席杨尚昆出席会议，做了题为“学习李四光”的重要讲话。

1999年10月26日，国土资源部、中国科学院、中国科协联合在北京召开纪念李四光诞辰110周年大会暨第六次李四光地质科学奖颁奖仪式和《中国地质学》（扩编版）首发式。中共中央政治局常委、国务院总理朱镕基对获奖的同志表示祝贺，中共中央政治局委员、国务院副总理温家宝出席纪念活动并讲话。

1989年10月26日在政协礼堂召开李四光诞辰100周年纪念大会。

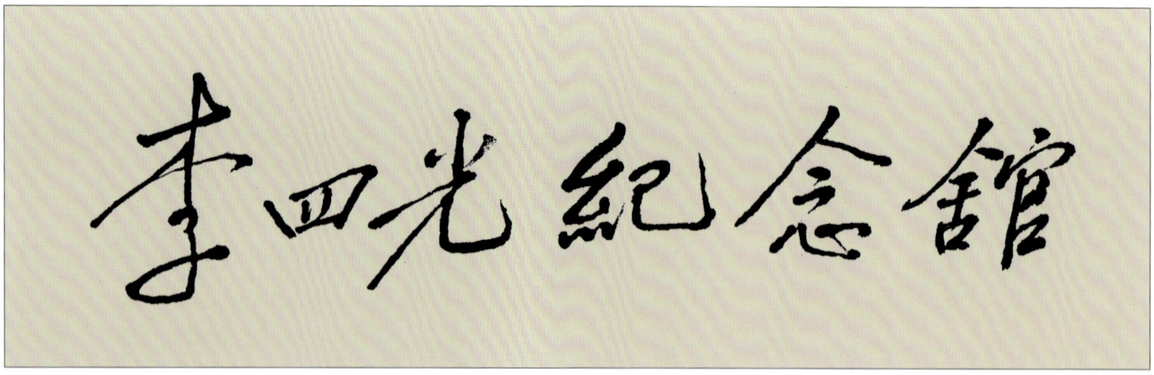

1989年国家主席李先念为李四光纪念馆题写馆名。

1989年李四光纪念馆在李四光故居揭幕。左一：程裕淇，左二：陈庆宣，
左五：周光召，左六：朱训（地质矿产部部长）。

2015年10月李四光纪念馆重新开放。

纪念馆西区外景（地质力学所科研楼）。

地质力学研究所院内李四光的铜像。

李四光纪念馆（故居）。

光辉足迹

李四光旧居光辉足迹主题内景。

卓越贡献主题内景。

事业传承主题内景。

精神永存主题内景。

1989年，我国设立了李四光地质科学奖，它是全国地质界最高荣誉奖，分荣誉奖、野外地质工作者奖、地质科技研究奖、地质教师奖和特别荣誉奖五类。

截至2024年9月，李四光地质科学奖自设立以来已经颁奖18次，共283人先后获奖，获奖者中有中国科学院及中国工程院两院院士、大专院校教授、工程技术人员和地质科学家。最高层次的荣誉奖一人只能授予一次，并作为终身荣誉奖。

李四光地质科学奖奖牌。

李四光地质科学奖外封。

主要参考文献

Main References

布莱克·威尔德，1922．中国和西伯利亚的石油资源［J］．美国矿冶工程师学会会报，68（2）．

陈群，张祥光，周国钧，等，1984．李四光传［M］．北京：人民出版社．

国立中央研究院文书处，1928．国立中央研究院十七年度总报告［R］．南京：国立中央研究院总办事处．

李四光，1928．燃料的问题［J］．现代评论，7（173）：8-12．

李四光，1933．䗴科分类标准及二叠纪七个新属［J］．中央研究院地质研究所西文集刊（14）：1-21．

李四光，1941．桂林科学实验馆概况［J］．建设研究，5（5）：5-8．

李四光，1951．庆祝中国共产党诞生三十周年［J］．科学通报，2（7）：691-692．

李四光，1956-04-05．在世界科协成立十周年纪念大会上的发言［N］．人民日报，3．

李四光，1957-06-25．党能领导科学工作［N］．人民日报，3．

李四光，1959．建国十年来中国地质工作的发展［J］．科学通报（18）：586－593．

李四光，1965．关于改进构造地质工作的意见［J］．地质评论，23（4）．

李四光，1965．关于地震地质工作问题［J］．中国地质（12）：5-6．

李四光，1974．萨尼（B. Sahni）纪念册［M］//李四光．区域地质构造分析．北京：科学出版社：65-82．

李四光，1975．中国第四纪冰川［M］．北京：科学出版社．

佚名，1958-06-26．松辽平原有石油［N］．人民日报，3．

佚名，1964-01-02．毛主席等领导人看豫剧《朝阳沟》［N］．人民日报，1．

佚名，1964-09-01. 北京科学讨论会胜利闭幕［N］. 人民日报，1.

中共中央文献研究室，1993. 周恩来经济文选［M］. 北京：中央文献出版社.

中共中央文献研究室，1997. 周恩来年谱（1949—1976）［M］. 北京：中央文献出版社.

中共中央文献研究室中央档案馆，2018. 建国以来周恩来文稿：第十三册［M］. 北京：中央文献出版社.

Lee J S，1939. The Geology of China. London：Thomas Murby：222.

图书在版编目（CIP）数据

李四光画传：第三版 /《李四光画传（第三版）》编辑组编. -- 北京：地质出版社, 2024. 10. -- ISBN 978-7-116-14290-9

Ⅰ. K826.14-64

中国国家版本馆CIP数据核字第2024KJ4193号

LI SIGUANG HUA ZHUAN（DI-SAN BAN）

责任编辑：罗军燕 王静怡
责任校对：关风云
出版发行：地质出版社
社址邮编：北京市海淀区学院路31号，100083
电　　话：（010）66554215(邮购部）；（010）66554540（编辑室）
网　　址：https://www.gph.clmpg.com
传　　真：（010）66554686
印　　刷：北京地大彩印有限公司
开　　本：889mm × 1194mm　1/16
印　　张：15.5
字　　数：200千字
版　　次：2024年10月北京第1版
印　　次：2024年10月北京第1次印刷
定　　价：196. 00元
书　　号：ISBN 978-7-116-14290-9